Faith's Pursuit

Published by
Deanna R. Slamans
324 Red Oak Lane
Hershey, PA 17033
(717) 982-5971

http://www.wix.com/dslamans/Faiths-Pursuit

ISBN: 978-0-578-02766-1

Cover Design by lulu.com

Printed in the United States of America

All Scripture quotations, unless otherwise indicated, are taken from the *New International Version.* Copyright © 1973, 1978, 1984 International Bible Society.

Faith's Pursuit

UNDERSTANDING GOD'S FAITHFULNESS IN SUFFERING

As I write this book, at the age of thirty-five, I am now the age of my mother when she died. This book is dedicated to her and to my seven year-old daughter who is the same age that I was at the time of the death of my mother.

I love you both…because I am both of you.

INTRODUCTION

When I first discovered the true, tangible meaning of faith, I was in a hotel room with my husband, Andy, our daughter Korri Faith and son, AJ. We had just spent the day at the Baltimore Inner Harbor's Aquarium and Discovery Zone and were heading to Richmond, Virginia to visit a former student who lived with us at the Milton Hershey School. We are full-time houseparents who take care of disadvantaged boys at a boarding school in Hershey, Pennsylvania. At any given time, our family lives with, on average, 12 teenage boys who are in need of care, financial support, and consistency as they grow into young men.

Because this was Spring Break, all of our students were home with their families of origin. We took this break to spend away from campus and to visit our student who was recently injured after his third tour of duty in Iraq. The injuries this young man sustained were alarming. He had returned to the United States paralyzed from an IED (improvised explosive device). We wanted to encourage him with our visit. Our plan was to make the visit the following day so after a few hours' drive we were able to locate a hotel just a few miles from the Virginia Veterans Administration (VA) Hospital.

Our children love a sleepover with their Mommy and Daddy. Even if they have to sleep on a hard hotel room floor or couch, they are just glad to be in the same room with us! As parents, we just hope that we get a good night's rest. When we snuggled down to sleep, I reached over to the nightstand for my Oswald Chambers devotional *My Utmost for His Highest*. I have read this book often enough during my walk with the Lord, but I still marvel at the ways that this amazing piece of work sustains me through my journey as a Christian.

On this particular evening, March 19, Chambers writes of *The Way of Abraham in Faith*[1] by telling the reader "faith never knows where it is being led, but it loves and knows the *One* who is leading. It is a life of faith, not of intellect and reason, but a life of knowing *Who* makes us go." He goes on to say that, one of the biggest snares to the Christian life is the idea that God is sure to lead us to success.

For me personally, the discovery of this myth was painful. For Abraham, I imagine it was as well. Especially when expectations of the Christian life seem unattainable (Abraham struggles with the timing of God's promise of a son), or when life wields its blows (God asks for Isaac as a sacrifice). However, Chambers reassures us when he describes the final stage of faith—pursuing God. This stage develops in long-suffering believers a special *character* that can only be attained by a life of walking and not fainting. It is not sanctification but more than that. It is a tried, and proved-true, journey with the One who is Faithful.

As I continued to read, God struck me with the realization that this Abraham, the father of the Hebrew nation, is the same father of *my* faith in God and *my* journey with Jesus Christ. God showed me—as He does many Biblical characters—what a life of faith looks like. In James 2:23, Abraham was called God's friend and was guaranteed a righteous deposit in Heaven because he was proven faithful. He believed God--He *long-suffered* with Him and it is for these reasons that I admire Abraham. Because I have experienced a large amount of suffering, I too am learning, like many other Heroes of the Faith, how to live out Hebrews 11:1-2...

Now faith is being sure of what you hope for and certain of what you do not see. This is what the ancients were commended for.

The ancients were admired greatly for this persistent pursuit of what it was that they were after. For Christians it is ultimately God, it is Jesus and it is the Holy Spirit. Up until that quiet night in the hotel room, when God spoke to the core of my being this profound truth, my Christian journey was largely comprised of myths.

I used to believe that my personal sufferings were because I did not grow up with a foundation of God in my life. I thought that I could never become a true woman of faith because I struggled with fear and doubt. For a long time, I did not believe that Christ *wanted* to do amazing things for me. With these false ideas as my baseline, I began to think that it was impossible to grow closer to the Lord.

On the contrary, as I look back at my most difficult moments with Jesus, I have appreciated that my most complicated tests of faith came when I least wished to see Christ's face. During those times, my faith journey was most lived out when I did not wish to be found by Him because my own failures and emotional hang-ups kept me hiding. I can remember moments when my spirit was so troubled that I could not even begin to know where to start looking for Him. Still, Christ sought **me** out…and *in faith,* I reached for His hand.

That evening, when the Lord spoke to me about the Christian life, He told me that Christianity is a *journey…not* a destination. My life's experiences do not sum up how God feels about me or what He has planned for me. God continues to show me that no matter what does not make sense about my life, or what He has allowed to happen in it, the constant pursuit of Christ is what true faith is.

It is my desire that you draw encouragement from this book through my life story and the biblical life profiles of some of the most profound "Failures of the Faith." They are failures by the world's standards, but they are truly the faithful ones in the eyes of God. Perhaps as you read this, you too will become convinced that God has called you forth to a journey of faith. When all else fails, the Christian journey is a life continually walking with God…and not fainting.

Part One

"God sets the lonely in families…" - Psalm 68:5-6

CHAPTER ONE

I was born *Deanna Rosetta Bradley* on Saturday, April 21, 1973. My middle name, *Rosetta*, came from my maternal grandmother whose name was Clarissa Rosetta Troutman and *Deanna* came from my father, Murrell Dean Bradley. He gave me the feminine version of his middle name. I was not alone when I came into the world because I had already a seven year-old sister. However, I did leave behind, in the uterus, a fraternal twin sister who was born exactly one hour after me. She was a lot smaller than I was and had to be fed intravenously because she was not able to eat properly for the first few days. One week later, our mom, Yvonne Eileen Bradley, brought us home from the hospital, where we lived in Chester, Pennsylvania for the first three years of our life.

Growing up with a twin sister was interesting. We dressed alike and people compared us constantly. I was considered the "quiet and reserved one" so my sister did the talking for me, and I was perfectly fine with that. Our differences were subtle because, for the most part, we liked the same things. We liked to read and were athletic. We did well in school when it came to academics. Nevertheless, our family situation during those formative years was chaotic and we were often in turmoil. As a result, my sister and I learned to cope, the best we could. Our relationship took on new meanings and forms as we navigated through each crisis together and sometimes alone.

A few years after our birth, our mother and father separated. When my father began displaying abnormal behavior, things took a turn for the worst. He complained of hearing voices and often saw things that other people did not. He was paranoid and responded to his fears in ways that upset the household. Our mother also battled her own mental illness. She had severe mood swings, and eventually took us children, and left him.

It happened one evening, while our father was out practicing with a music group that he performed with on the weekends. Normally our mother would have gone to practice with him because she liked singing with his band during their rehearsals; but that evening she did not go. Instead, she packed our things and took us away to the western part of the state. My dad returned home to find us gone. He did not know when he left for practice, that it would be the last time that he would ever see his wife. I do not have a family picture of all of us. I do not even remember us all together in the same home. This was the beginning of what would become a wound so large that only Christ would be able to heal it.

We moved to a western Pennsylvania town located about an hour east of Pittsburgh. After a few years, we moved in with our maternal grandmother who lived in the "projects". My grandmother was a heavy drinker, which added to the shaky foundation of our upbringing. We were poor, and although all of these things were part of my early childhood, I have fond memories of my mother and grandmother simply because they were the ones taking care of me. Throughout our toddler years, my twin sister and I bounced from various family members' homes when my mother's emotional needs grew severe.

Bipolar disorder makes an otherwise normal person's mood swings often unbearable. My mother's strong highs and deep lows were not always easy to deal with. She took medication for it at times, but she said that it made her feel "spacey"—especially after she had us twins. During different times of the year, her mood would change. Her mania made her the most energetic, happiest, and busiest mother on the block, but during her low points her energy went into feeding thoughts of suicide because she could not bear the thought of what it took to survive. Eventually her mood swings changed so frequently that it grew increasingly difficult to predict her mental state.

Although she took medicine sporadically, her condition grew worse. She tried to take her life numerous times during my early years because her depression was so severe. Her final attempt happened on the evening of August 25, 1980. Someone discovered her body beneath one of the bridges of the small town where we lived. She had a fractured jaw, and one of her legs was broken in several places. She was unconscious. It took several months for her to recover from her many injuries and for five months, she remained in the hospital before unexpectedly going into a coma. One month after that, she suffered a stroke and died. The day was January 12, 1981, and I was seven years old.

My world came crashing down.

For a little girl, a mother's existence is the strongest source of her identity, reflection, and self-worth. Regardless of her faults, our mother's confidence was our security, her happiness our peace—and her death our terrible heart break. When our mother died that cold, winter day, I believe that something inside me, and each one of my sisters, died as well. Only a few short months after our mother passed away, our grandmother did as well. On May 23, of that same year, the heavy drinking took a toll on her body and her liver stopped working. Even at that young age, I knew that our life was turning out to be a very bad situation.

That summer, we bounced around to extended family, on our mother's side, who took us in. Our cousins, aunts, and uncles were gentle and kind and gave us the comfort and distraction that we needed to get through those very difficult months. Then, one hot day, my father's oldest sister came to our small town to claim us. We drove three hours east to the big city of Harrisburg, PA. She took us to her home to raise us as her own. Even though it was a lot of change in a short period, I knew it was necessary for us to have some stability. It soon proved to be a passing wish on a long list of dreams for me that seemed to never come true.

~~~~~~

One day during the first winter after our move to Harrisburg, my sisters and I were walking home from an after school activity in the neighborhood. As we traveled the few blocks to the house, I started to cross the street with them but instead ran out into it without looking and was struck by a car. I was thrown ten feet in the air and I landed hard on the hood--I was nearly killed. I suffered a broken leg and arm, and had a severe head injury. I was bleeding internally—organs were damaged, and I was rushed to the emergency room for surgery. It was December 10, 1981.

After two months in the hospital, I was sent home in a body cast. At eight years-old I was wrapped in plaster from waist to toe on my right leg and waist to knee on my left. My arm was in a cast as well. The doctors had wrapped a large bandage around my head. While recovering at home, I stayed in a hospital bed in the front room of the house and could not get up even to use the bathroom. I spent that first winter and Christmas recovering.

Fortunately, I did not fall behind too much in school because every afternoon, my third grade teacher came to bring me my schoolwork. She also tutored me a few days a week after school. Recovery was slow but progressive and it looked hopeful that by spring, I would be walking again. I did not know why, but God had spared my life.

The atmosphere at home grew worse during that time as accusations between my aunt and older sister mounted over whose "fault" it was that a car hit me. I knew the fault was my own because I did not look both ways before crossing the street—but no one else seemed to want to blame me. Tempers flared between them, and I watched them fight from my hospital bed, helpless to break it up. My twin sister and I could do nothing to stop them from harming each other. Then the unthinkable happened--my older sister was asked to leave the house.

That evening, she called family on our mother's side that lived in Detroit, and by the next morning, she had gone out there to be with them. My twin sister and I lived the rest of our childhood without her and her loss was felt tremendously those first few years. Our older sister signified a stable force in our life. What she provided for my twin and I was priceless. She had been a mother to us when our mom and grandmother were dealing with their personal issues. Many times, she stepped in to be the strength we needed. We depended on her more than I had realized and her departure was overwhelming. This was another unbearable loss that I was not prepared to deal with.

My twin sister began to have nightmares from witnessing the car accident when I was knocked into the air. Even though I was healing quicker than the doctors had anticipated, she still feared that she would somehow lose me, too. We grew very dependent on each other for our continued existence. It was an unhealthy dependency but one that helped us to manage.

With so much loss in such a short period, I began to withdraw. I did not know how to grieve any of what was taking place. How could I? Losing a mother, grandmother, and sister within the span of one year was too much to process at eight years old. As I grew quieter, I also grew afraid of attaching to anyone. Slowly, I built a wall of bricks around my fragile heart—I did not let anyone in for a very long time.

My twin and I attended the city schools in Harrisburg from third to seventh grade, and thankfully had not had much change during those years. We were grateful for the consistency because our souls were weary. I loved school and made good grades. I did what I was told, and I rarely misbehaved. My quiet little heart was guarded and even though I made a few friends, the friendships were not deep. I rarely expressed my emotions except through tears when I was alone.

On the contrary, my sister acted out her pain in school and on the playground. She was often in conflict with people—adults and peers alike. She fought others to deal with life and her poor behavior in and out of school eventually became a source of shame for her and me. I eventually played the role of peacemaker, trying to get her to see things differently and thinking of ways to get her out of the trouble she often made for herself. But, her negative behavior increased, and as a result, I closed up even more because of the conflict I witnessed in her life. I no longer wanted to be a part of her pain because I could barely deal with my own.

As we attended elementary and junior high school we learned more and more about what happened to our father after we left him in Chester, PA. Shortly after our mother moved us, our father left Chester to work down south. He picked tobacco in the fields around his extended family's land in North Carolina. Although he was still battling his mental illness, he went to work and made a living from what the soil yielded.

After a few years, his paranoia grew worse and eventually, my father ended up in prison for stabbing a man to death. On November 15, 1979, the state charged him with manslaughter and sentenced him to 8-12 years. This was a reduced sentence from the mandatory 20 years for manslaughter in North Carolina, because the 9-1-1 tape contained a recording of my father's call to the paramedics. Apparently, after the stabbing, he called to get the man some help. He also worked to revive him but eventually failed to save his life. This bit of information was impressive to the judge during the sentencing hearing, thus he received half of what the law allowed for in 1979.

Behind bars, my father received a formal diagnosis of paranoid schizophrenia—*with homicidal tendencies*. He began the long road to treatment and served out his sentence often heavily medicated and disoriented. My twin sister and I went to visit him every summer during his incarceration, not fully understanding the extent of his crime or his mental state.

He felt like a stranger to me because our contact with him was only two hours on one summer day, each calendar year. We joined him for a picnic on the prison grounds, usually on a Saturday, bringing buckets of Kentucky Fried Chicken with us. Many of the prisoners' families did the same. He commented about how tall we were getting and told me that I was looking more and more like Yvonne—his beloved wife. His words were affectionate, but I no longer knew this man and my heart grew apart from him.

CHAPTER TWO

My father's sister faithfully cared for us in his absence, working hard and saving her money so that we were able to have whatever we needed. Bills were paid on time and there was always plenty of food in the house. Christmas times were memorable and traditions were developing for us as a family—as fragmented as it was. Overall, things progressed normally throughout our junior high years. We learned to do chores and to take care of our things properly. Our aunt was a strict woman and she was not to be disrespected. We learned quickly the consequences for doing so. Often, my sister and I felt that as long as we had each other, things would work out fine—and they were fine for a long time.

When my father returned from prison, I was almost 12 years old. It was 1984 and I still did not realize the amount of treatment he was under for his schizophrenia. We were not told that he had a mental illness. He was heavily medicated when he first came home and we did not understand his need to sleep so often. He also had a bad back from a herniated disc, so he would lie down frequently to help ease the pain. He was adjusting to life outside of an institution so he maintained habits that a prisoner would maintain. In those early months home he rarely left the house except to smoke out on the front porch.

He could not work until he was mentally stable and acclimated again to regular life. I thought he acted strangely so I limited the amount of time I interacted with him, but he and my sister got into conflict often. Their tempers were equally matched, it seemed. I watched, silently, as they made the harsh adjustment of getting to know one another again. Because our father missed a great deal of our childhood, it was difficult for us to learn to respect him.

One year after my father came home; our aunt enrolled my sister and me in a boarding school in Hershey, Pennsylvania. It was called the Milton Hershey School and, to me, going there was a dream come true. The school is for kids who have had a very stressful upbringing, were financially poor, and either one or no parents to care for them. Milton Hershey, the genius who invented the great American chocolate bar, started the school for orphans boys in 1909 and left his entire fortune to the school in 1918—a grand total of sixty million dollars!

Already in the eighth grade when we enrolled, my sister and I were easy to care for. We were perfect candidates for the school because our mother was dead and our father was not our primary caregiver. I did not mind the move to Hershey, where the air often smelled like chocolate from the nearby chocolate factory. I also did not mind living in a very large house, called a student home, with thirteen other girls my same age.

The chores were simple enough, and the long hours spent outdoors in the grass and trees were a welcome treat to our former life of public housing and noisy, urban streets. I even milked cows during my high school years! Strangely enough, when we enrolled at the school and met our middle school houseparents and the other girls in the home, for the first time in my life I felt like I was *home!*

I do not believe that my twin sister shared as many good sentiments about the school as I did. She was still trying to figure out how to get along with others. She continued to get into conflict with classmates, roommates and the houseparents who took care of us. Group living proved not to match with her personality. Her pain spoke louder than anything else did about her and the trouble that she was in, seemed endless. Perhaps she was not able to handle yet another life change.

On the contrary, I stayed out of trouble most of the time but her negative behavior still affected me enormously. I took on her shame and guilt. Her trouble was my own and my heart ached for her. I spent many days defending her and begging her not to talk back or argue so that she would not find herself in trouble again.

Halfway through our ninth grade year, my sister moved to another student home for a fresh start. However, within weeks, she was in conflict again and I heard rumors that she could possibly be terminated from the school. I was not able to talk to her everyday as I had before so it was hard to give her the encouragement she needed. As I feared, she was not in her student home long before our aunt was asked to come and take her home. Her time at the Milton Hershey School was over.

I was suddenly all alone.

Even though there were a dozen or so other girls in the home and a set of houseparents, along with their two biological children, there was no one left from my family of origin. I did not want to feel this unexpected disappointment because it was too great. The wall I built around my heart years earlier was holding firm. Loss was becoming familiar to me and I grew numb to it.

Instead of feeling the void from my twin's absence, I forged ahead busying myself with sports, music performances, and outside activities because they were a welcomed distraction from the pain. By graduation, I had become the "model" MHS student, involved in many things and keeping my grades up. However, I had not even begun to deal with my problems.

In those days, I believe I coped well because God helped shield me from the pain of everything. I know that I would not have made it through those days otherwise. Sociologists call children who make it through insurmountable odds a resilient child—but frankly, I simply survived. I did not feel resilient then and, 20 years later, I still do not feel resilient. I feel blessed and called forth for a purpose; and perhaps that is the sole reason for my tragic life.

In the book of Job there is a conversation documented between the Lord and Satan over the fate of Job's life. Satan asks for permission to "try" Job, so that he is proven unfaithful to God. Yet Job remains humble even as he pursues and questions the Lord's plans for him. In the beginning of the 38th chapter, he finally receives an answer, and through his conversation with God, Job reaches a point where he realizes that he is but dust and that the Lord is indeed sovereign...even in the midst of a person's suffering. Job proves even more faithful in the face of his tragedies. In the beginning of chapter 42, he says to God, "I *know that you can do all things; no plan of yours can be thwarted...my ears had heard of you but now my eyes have seen you."*

This acceptance of God's sovereignty becomes evident only to saints who do not grow bitter from life's difficult circumstances. They inquire of the Lord and He answers them. The answers are not easy and sometimes they do not make sense, but through time He shows His purpose and His plan will always go forth.

As a child of God, when I had come to the end of myself--I had finally reached the beginning of God, and, like Job, it was an awful and wonderful place to be. I learned that only then, could the Lord pick me up and do something with me.

During my childhood, I did not have knowledge of God in a strong way. I did not know much about Him to reject Him in my anger. I also do not think that God was "testing" me as He did Job during those early years—though, my test would come years later. I do believe, however, that during those troubling times, God was purposefully moving me in and out of situations to protect me from further future harm. I know this seems strange because I experienced a lot of pain in those early years, but they pale in comparison to what might have taken place had certain situations remained the same or if I had not attended the Milton Hershey School.

In Jeremiah 29:11, we find an amazing statement from the Lord that I have personalized for myself whenever I am faced with a circumstance that is unbearably difficult to deal with. The Lord says, *"For I know the plans I have for you...plans to prosper you and not to harm you. Plans to give you a hope and a future."*

In other words, God is the author of my life and He wrote my life story—as dreadful as it is. God's plans for me are for my well-being. He knew what He was doing when he allowed my mother to take her life, my grandmother to die from too much drinking, and my car accident to occur. He knew what He was doing when He allowed my older sister to be raised by another family, and for my twin sister to eventually move to another state. He also knew what He was doing when He allowed me to stand on my own—alone at 15 years old. Twenty years later, God still knows what He is doing as He wills and works out the past hurts and disappointments in my life, to continue to refine my shattered heart.

I have grown to trust Him daily as He does this.

CHAPTER THREE

The Milton Hershey School proved to be the pivotal point in the development of the remainder of my childhood. As I watched my houseparents care for the girls and me, I realized that for the first time in my life I saw a married couple interact on a daily basis. No one abandoned us girls, or left me. I was encouraged by my own talents, as I learned to sing and play an instrument, act on stage, and participate in sports. My houseparents, along with my aunt and Dad, came to many of my performances. Days turned into weeks and weeks into months as I lived my new life at that wonderful place. Nearing the end of my eighth grade year, I was having the time of my life and it seemed that I had just arrived yesterday.

With so many good things going on during that first year at MHS, by far, the best thing that ever happened to me was the night that I gave my heart to the Lord Jesus Christ. Our houseparents had asked earlier that afternoon if any of us were interested in going to a Christian concert. Having never been to one, I decided to go out of curiosity and I was so happy that I did.

The *Glad* concert was held in a local school auditorium. I had never heard an *a capella* group sing before and as I sat there, I noticed that there were no instruments set up, only four microphones beneath a soft spotlight . As soon as the group was introduced, four men came out and began to sing, and as they did, my heart was carried away to another place.

Their voices sounded like instruments and the tight harmony drew me into worship. They affectionately sang about Jesus and I suddenly became keenly aware of Him and His supreme existence. I had so much going on in my life up until that point that I never took the time to seek Him out—but He knew where I was. He always did—and that evening I found Him. After the concert, I came forward and prayed a prayer with some people who were lined up in front of the stage. I gave my heart to Jesus and was told to read the Bible, pray, and seek Him daily. I knew then that I desperately needed Him to help me through so many things. Because of that evening, the rest of my young adult years turned out to be dramatically different. I had joined God's family and was never the same!

As a scared young woman who had been through so many devastating circumstances, I realized that I needed to cling to God because if I did not, I thought certainly that I would die. In fact, I had died emotionally many times prior to being introduced to Him. With each loss, heartbreak, and disappointment I experienced as a child a little part of me was destroyed. The trust that I had had about life and the dreams of doing great things had become passing fancies, until that fateful night.

What drew me to the cross was not only the idea that I was a sinner in need of saving, but simply the idea that I needed saving—from my own self and whatever further fate was in store. Prior to becoming a Christian, I had not dealt with any of the pain from my disappointments. How could I even begin to? There was no safe place to turn or anyone with whom to talk. In fact, I had not talked to anyone about my hurts before.

But, then I began to talk to God. I wrote in my journal religiously--at first just to get my feelings out. I told Him everything. I told Him my thoughts and feelings about life, but I primarily told Him my hurts and loneliness. I discovered after a short while that what I really needed was for Christ to come, pick me up and hold me for while—and He did just that. I began reading His word and found tremendous comfort from its pages.

My houseparents demonstrated to me the love of Christ as they raised me. When I made mistakes, they were patient and taught me through understanding and discipline. When I needed emotional support, they provided it with no strings attached. I did not feel judgment from them, but rather godly encouragement and guidance.

Throughout my high school years at the Milton Hershey School, I became involved in many things. I advanced as a clarinet player, sang in the choir, and competed onstage with the drama team. I became a member of the National Honors Society; the school's Leadership Team and was Vice-President and President of our student home. I ran cross-country and track, took the statistics for the Varsity Basketball team, and joined the Jazz Band and Jazz Choir (called New Horizons). I even wrote for the school's newspaper. The world opened up for me in so many ways. I believe it was because I heard the Lord's voice to trust Him as I attended that school and to allow Him to work in my life through the loving people who worked there. I was not disappointed.

Proudly, I graduated from the Milton Hershey School on Sunday, June 3, 1991. It was the happiest and yet saddest day of my life. I knew that I was going to miss that place because it was the first time, on a daily basis, that it felt good to be alive. Surprisingly, in that busy student home and school I felt more like myself than I ever did before I attended there. I also knew, for the first time, that I could be proud of myself and my achievements--and that I mattered!

~~~~~~

My houseparents had given me the sound advice to attend a Christian college--especially because I lacked spiritual discipline and basic Biblical knowledge. It seemed the logical thing to do in order to grow in my faith. Academically, I earned Milton Hershey School's continuing education scholarship as well as many other grants that helped me graduate from Messiah College without taking out a single loan.

I was eager to get to know other Christians and to learn all that I could about what it meant to live a life of faith even in the midst of my suffering. I also wanted to get involved in ministry and, though I felt inadequate, I discovered that I could sing well enough to be selected for one of the campus' music ministry teams. I learned to sing with four or five other members of the ensemble; and to share my "testimony", or life story, at churches in the surrounding area.

It felt awkward at first sharing with strangers the many losses that I had experienced in my childhood. I was convinced that the people in the congregation would react negatively to my childhood traumas. After sharing my testimony, I usually sang a song by Twila Paris called, *Do I Trust You, Lord?* A song that spoke to my heart just as much as it did to the others who heard it. Many in the audience cried as I spoke and sang. I was surprised that they grieved my losses along with me. It was an amazing feeling to be able to point others to a loving God because of the brokenness in my life.

I truly felt that I had discovered my purpose while at Messiah. I continued to serve on the music ministry team throughout my freshman and sophomore years, and I got involved in some of the theatrical productions at the college. My confidence soared as I discovered a great way to give back to God what He had given to me—a redeemed life!

Things went well those first few years and I learned a lot about Christian "culture" and mainstream Christianity. I met people whose entire life experience encompassed the church. They had known God's word ever since they could speak! I loved that I could learn about God's word in and out of the classroom and it was refreshing for me to be able to attend chapel a few days a week. I was glad to be part of a body of believers and it was wonderful to grow in God's larger family of Christians.

Yet, even though I was a fellow believer, I felt like an outsider because I was new in my faith and still had a lot of growing to do. I also knew that many of the students at Messiah College did not come from families like mine and that I was a survivor embarking on a journey mostly alone. As a result, their "comfortable" lives were foreign to me and I had a difficult time relating to my fellow classmates.

I soon found myself missing the city and the needy people there. I knew that I could identify with whom the Bible calls "outcasts" and I believed that I felt a tug on my heart to serve those in desperate need. Knowing what Jesus could do with my shattered life made the desire to serve others like me grow stronger. Soon that need was fulfilled because an opportunity presented itself, that I absolutely could not refuse.

As a Communications major; the more that I sang and performed on stage, the more I grew to love the performing arts as much as I did writing. With that in mind, during the second semester of my sophomore year, I switched my major to Radio, TV & Film and the completion of it required me to finish my degree at the Messiah-Philly Campus located in the heart of Philadelphia, Pennsylvania. I moved there that summer.

I was glad to be returning to the city, because I missed city life. Going to the Milton Hershey School provided a wonderful reprieve from the harsh streets and public housing that I had grown used to. Nevertheless, I missed the flavor and noise of the city and was glad to be back in it. I had become isolated during my first two years at Messiah College's main campus because my feelings of inadequacy still plagued me. In fact, my insecurities increased there because I was one of the few students who did not grow up in a Christian home or attend a Christian school. The poverty that was apparent in the few blocks surrounding Temple University's campus felt more familiar to me than the rolling green hills on the outskirts of Harrisburg.

In Philadelphia, I found a church that soon became my lifeline as I navigated the city. It was located in the absolute worst part of North Philadelphia. *The Badlands*, as was nicknamed by "60 Minutes" when they aired their urban violence and poverty special, is located in the Kensington area of North Philadelphia. The neighborhood is a cross-section of Blacks, Whites, and Hispanics living together in one community. It was a difficult place to see God work because drugs and violence were widespread and it appeared to be a hopeless place to do ministry.

As I attended one of the neighborhood churches, I learned that many of the adults or older males who lived in this neighborhood were often abusive to the young girls growing up there. At young ages, the girls would run away and eventually sell themselves on the street to make a living. They had believed a devastating lie—that their only significance came from performing sexual acts for money.

Most of the young men grew up believing that selling drugs and behaving violently was the only true path to manhood. Empty lives that ended too soon left shadows behind in the form of murals spray-painted on the sides of abandoned buildings. I looked in wonder at these paintings that honored the dead who were killed in drug-related incidents. The artwork is impeccable.

The church that I grew to love and rely on during the remainder of my college years was a bright light in that dark place. It was mostly known for its men's drug rehab program. Men who recently returned from incarceration, or who struggled with drug addictions could sign into the program and live at the church. Ironically, I felt a type of connection with these men because I knew that somehow, in that church, I was accepted even amidst my failures and shortcomings.

Seeing volunteers, missionaries, and the pastoral staff work with these men as they battled their addictions, gave me comfort. I knew then that the people in that church were not afraid of my raw emotions and deep spiritual hunger. Many in the congregation had grown up as I had—from a broken home and from tragic circumstances. It was truly a place that I could receive ministry. I also felt that I had something to offer in return. I will forever be grateful to Bethel Temple Community Bible Church for its authentic ministry to the lonely and hurting.

During my first summer in Philadelphia, I lived in an apartment above the church. Because I had no "home", I sought housing there. In exchange for room and board, I worked on various projects around the church building. These ranged from cooking and cleaning to painting and even assisting the pastor with stage sets for the church's annual plays and productions. I also helped with the summer kids' camps and the street ministries. I loved serving Christ in that holy place because I was reminded daily of people's needs, along with my own, and, ironically, it was what helped me stay encouraged.

In the summer, an urban church is a very active place. With day camps for children set up on abandoned open lots, and outreach events held on various street corners, there was no time for sitting around. In the evenings, once a week, street meetings were held on the toughest of these corners.

The senior pastor selected volunteers and he put together a special ministry team. These nighttime gatherings were called Open-Air Meetings and the team traveled every Tuesday night to a different violent street corner all over the Kensington area.

When the pastor learned that I could sing and share my testimony he asked me to attend a street meeting one evening and I was excited to join the team. After a gripping, pre-meeting prayer time held in the church basement, volunteers gathered up gospel tracts and sound equipment to load into the church van. Armed with water bottles, to keep hydrated in the city's late afternoon heat, and walking shoes, we traveled the city blocks to the chosen street corner in preparation to begin canvassing the neighborhood.

The volunteers on the team were made up of some of the most unlikely people to do ministry. First, there was me, then at least one or two ex-drug dealers or ex-gang members, a sprinkling of women who had received the grace of Christ years earlier from a long life of addiction or abuse, and other faithful servants of Christ who had grown up around the church and its neighborhood. I admired these volunteers because, despite all that they had been through, their hearts were eager to obey the call of God to go and share the Good News. I was honored to be a part of the team.

I discovered after my first meeting how the pastor chose the street corner where he would minister each week. He based his selection on the most violent crime that had recently occurred in the neighborhood. Many times these incidents went unreported by the news media so it was crucial for him to keep his ear to the streets and investigate the latest gossip. At first, I did not quite understand why it mattered where our meetings were held, but then I witnessed an amazing transformation my first evening on the team.

We canvassed the neighborhood by walking a grid of two-to-three blocks around the selected corner inviting folks to come to the street meeting at the named intersection. Sometimes the yellow police tape from the recent crime was still hanging from the utility poles flapping lazily in the hot summer breeze as our sound crew hooked up the equipment and unraveled thick extension cords. Folks grew curious watching our team set up the stage. But, mostly the neighborhood activity continued without much notice. Drug dealing hardly missed a beat while curious kids watched our crew hook up microphones and speakers as they played amongst broken glass and trash.

When we invited neighbors on the block to come hear some music and an encouraging word, I saw the emptiness in people's eyes and the pain that shown in their faces, as they grieved in that neighborhood. There was always a strong sense of urgency when we communicated the upcoming evening meeting. I was amazed that we did not need to hang flyers or make announcements far in advance. We simply invited the people from the block to come—and often they would.

Sometimes as we canvassed the streets, I had a fellow church member with me who spoke Spanish because I could not. On those evenings, I simply handed out tracts to those who could not understand my English and I smiled as they conversed in a foreign language, their strange voices penetrating the evening air.

During the Open Air meetings, it became apparent to me that the senior pastor's gift was evangelism. He loved to share the gospel to the downcast and broken-hearted. Along with his many duties of preaching and teaching the body of believers, he designed stage sets for theatrical productions and visited members and other struggling families on a weekly basis. However, what he did on Tuesday nights at the Open-Air meetings was nothing short of a miracle. I saw lives transformed when there was no more hope. Light shined in the young people's eyes again when they had grown dark from the pain of living in this damaged world. Hearts were forever changed.

I have to admit, that even though I knew that the Lord was orchestrating these divine meetings on those hot and humid nights, I was still nervous and often afraid on those street corners sharing the Gospel. Many times as I spoke about how the Lord had changed my life and become the Comforter of my soul, the drug dealing continued. Sometimes a drunk would holler out or a disturbed person mocked the meeting in a loud voice, but I managed to stay on track with what I was saying. I followed up my testimony with a song. By then I had added *Beauty for Ashes* by Crystal Lewis and a few selections from Babbie Mason to my song repertoire. Some nights our teenage drama troupe performed a mime or dramatic selection that I helped direct.

After the song or drama, the pastor would set up his easel and bright paints and preach a simple gospel message to the onlookers in the crowd. He used ultraviolet lights to shine on his canvas, and as the sun set, his paintings would glow on the page. He spoke both English and Spanish, alternating between the two languages as he frantically painted an illustration onto the canvas. Initially the activity on the corner continued, but without fail, about halfway through the message a hush would fall over the street corner as the Holy Spirit quietly did His work. Parents and older siblings gathered their children close and the drug dealing ceased. Neighbors would stop oncoming cars and ask drivers to turn down their music as they slowly passed, so that everyone could hear the message. Many times, I heard weeping as conviction fell on some and a sense of hope fell on others.

On those sacred Tuesday nights, I marveled at the way the Holy Spirit ministered to so many different hearts a message that was specifically for each individual. What happened next never ceased to amaze me. Different people in the crowd stepped forward to respond to the call of Christ. Some of them were battling AIDS; others bore tattoos and scars from gang initiations and violent crimes. Even still, prayers were prayed and lives were changed. Addicts were set free and those abused or molested began the slow process of healing. Death was present on those violent streets, but our desire was to bring Life to that awful place. Whenever I learned of someone's enormous need, I shuddered in amazement, perhaps because I knew that God allowed me to be intimately involved in His *kingdom work* and I was awestruck by its power.

As we ministered those summers in that tremendously complex and hopeless city, I was reminded of a passage from Isaiah 58. In it, the Lord is challenging His people to a life of ministry where their time spent fasting matches the Lord's heart for his hurting people. When I first read the verses I could not make sense of how fasting related to God's ministry to the oppressed, but as I began this intense life of ministering to wounded people on a daily basis, it all began to resonate with me in my spirit.

"Is not this the kind of fasting I have chosen: to loose the chains of injustice and untie the cords of the yoke, to set the oppressed free and break every yoke? Is it not to share your food with the hungry and to provide the poor wanderer with shelter—when you see the naked, to clothe him, and not to turn away from your own flesh and blood?" -- Isaiah 58:5-7

Pouring myself out through ministry was not only a great way to give back to the Lord, but it was also healing for my thirsty soul. Later on in this same passage, the Lord gives this healing promise to those who empty themselves for the sake of others.

Then your light will break forth like the dawn, and your healing will quickly appear; then your righteousness will go before you, and the glory of the Lord will be your rear guard. Then you will call, and the Lord will answer; you will cry for help and he will say: Here am I...The Lord will guide you always; he will satisfy your needs in a sun-scorched land and will strengthen your frame...You will be called Repairer of Broken Walls, Restorer of Streets with Dwellings..." Isaiah 58: 8-9, 11, & 12b.

The Gospel of Christ is scandalous to those who believe that Christ died for a neat world. He can be an obstacle to the most pious and religious people because of how much they limit His power. They believe that there are places in this world where He will not go. Surprisingly, the raw suffering that comes from impoverished neighborhoods and broken homes is where you *will* find Christ's heart. He is often there in those streets because He is the only hope in that devastated place. Although the darkness of my upbringing mirrored the darkness of the city, what drew me to minister there week after week, year after year, was the knowledge that Christ was and still is the hope for so many broken people. I grew to love and adore Christ's church for the healing that it brought to my soul and the family that it became for me during those early years as a young believer.

CHAPTER FOUR

Working in Philadelphia that first year, gave me the opportunity to see many aspects of urban church ministry. There seemed always to be more work than workers. Sometimes, because a more important crisis was at hand, regular church work was delayed. Urban ministry is often complicated and hard work, but I did not care because I knew that it was something that I felt destined to be a part.

I am not sure when the specific call to youth ministry came to me, but the tug on my heart to work with hurting teens was persistent. I did not know that it would later become my life's work. I had not even heard of youth ministry prior to coming to Messiah College, but one day, while reading the book of Isaiah, I felt that I had reached a place where God could use me.

In Isaiah 6:1-8 the prophet's commission is at hand. Isaiah has just seen a vision of the Lord seated on His throne and the Heavenly creatures who often accompany Him in the scriptures. The creatures are calling out to one another testifying of the Lord's holiness. Their voices caused the doorposts and thresholds to shake as the temple filled with smoke.

"Woe is me!" Isaiah cried. "I am ruined! For I am a man of unclean lips and I live among a people of unclean lips, and my eyes have seen the King, the Lord Almighty."

Then one of the winged creatures flew over to him with a hot burning lump of coal. He touched Isaiah's lips with it and told him that his sins were atoned for. His sins are forgiven and his redemption came. As I continued to read, it dawned on me that Isaiah received his redemption only *after* he admitted his complete and utter destruction before a Holy God. The Lord then asked Isaiah whom He should send and who was willing to go. Isaiah knew immediately that this was a call to his heart and he willingly cried out for the Lord to send him as His vessel. Isaiah did not become frozen in condemnation because he knew that this makes a saint useless to the Lord. Neither did He allow himself to become consumed with his inadequacy. He chose to believe the Redeemer of his soul—Jesus, rather than the *accuser* of it—Satan. Isaiah knew who was calling Him and he humbly accepted the work.

Another saint who experienced an unexpected commission was Moses. Only after his life came to a grinding halt did it prove effective to the Lord. As an infant, he was handpicked by God and was called out by name to free God's people, but after he took the liberation of the children of Israel into his own hands things took a very different turn. Moses was so desperate to see his people unchained that he killed a man; and this haunted him repeatedly. He was forced to flee from the only land he had ever known. However, many years later, humbled by the choices he had made, Moses still had a heart for God because he had never stopped listening for Him. When the Lord finally spoke to Moses, he knew without a doubt, that he was indeed still the chosen one. He too decided to listen to His Redeemer and put to rest the voice that had accused him all those years.

Moses' failures could have stopped him from hearing God's voice. Countless Christians, myself included, who were convinced of a word from God or a call on their heart for ministry, abandon it because of mistakes made or life circumstances gone wrong. Discouragement sets in when failures take awhile to repair. Even still, the Lord chooses whom He will to do His work and we are not to ask why, but to simply obey and go. What He wants to do is for *His* glory not our own. At times, it does not make sense, but God will often use those of us who are tattered and worn from life's battles to do His work.

What we see in Scripture is a God who seeks out a person for His work and He often calls them forth when the person least expects it. When God orchestrates our trials and shows us His faithfulness, we see our utter dependency on Him. Yet we are still able to stand before His Holiness when we place our feeble trust in Him. Only then are we truly useful for His kingdom work.

~~~~~~

As a youth worker, I worked alongside some of the most encouraging, faithful saints of God; whom I discovered were also some of the humblest people that I have ever known. Their journeys with God were not deterred by the inconveniences of life because many of them had been through the worst of circumstances. They were survivors. These youth workers and leaders in the church knew what it meant to cry out to a distant God and discover that He is a lot closer than things appear—because even through their trials they had learned to keep listening for Him. They shared with me amazing stories of triumph through their tragedies, and I loved to hear their stories because they fueled my faith.

It was with these incredible volunteers that I began my service to the Lord in youth ministry. I had done previous work with teens at Christian summer camps prior to those years in Philadelphia, but this was before the call to youth was clear to me. Frankly, I worked at camps primarily because the job provided me housing and food between college semesters when I had nowhere else to live. It was also a wonderful way to make money and enjoy kids in a relaxed outdoor setting.

I found out quickly that urban youth ministry is a different story altogether. Because their lives were often chaotic, it proved to be a combination of social work, crisis intervention, and good old-fashioned relational youth ministry. When kids needed us, we were there. Youth group meetings took place once a week and were a great way to give kids a safe place to go for fun when the streets were unsafe. As a youth volunteer, I helped design skits and silly games to "hook" the kids in before the message was given.

Sitting around the room in our youth center were kids who were hurting badly and desperately needed to know that someone in their concrete jungle cared for them. I could relate well to those kids because many of their backgrounds were similar to mine. Their pain was very real to me because as a twenty year-old, I was just beginning to work through my own. There were others, however, whose lives were far worse than I ever imagined a child's could be, and whenever I was fortunate enough to gain their trust, these kids would share the source of their pain and I was stunned that they had made it this far.

One particular evening, while we were planning an outing for a winter retreat, a visitor joined the meeting in the youth center that was located across the street from the church. He was a fellow youth worker who did volunteer work at a church in the suburbs of Philadelphia while he finished his last college semester. The first thing that I noticed about this young man was his smile. His eyes sparkled when he laughed and he had an amazing way of making everyone in the room feel special. He listened intently when others spoke. Later that evening, after he left, I asked about him to one of the volunteers who seemed to know him well, and I learned that he was from Chicago and was attending Eastern College located in St. Davids, PA-- just a half hour's drive out of the city. His major was Youth Ministry and he minored in Social Work. His name was Andy Slamans.

The result of the meeting was a decision to have a portion of our winter retreat at Andy's school. It was our desire to take the kids out of the city for the weekend. Andy helped us design a scavenger hunt at Eastern College because he knew the campus well. The staff helped design the riddles while Andy provided the prizes for the winners.

Armed with clues written on 3x5 cards and a group of loud Hispanic, Black and White teens, our youth group traipsed through the winter landscape as the sun was setting.

We wore hats, gloves, puffy coats, and boots because of the recent snowfall. An hour later, when there were no more clues to be found, we made our way indoors for some hot chocolate, and to watch the guys play a late night game of basketball.

As I began to climb the small hill that lead to the gymnasium and cafeteria, I slipped and fell with my face planted in the cold, wet snow. I got up quickly to brush the snow off my knees, face, and hands and noticed a black-gloved hand reaching out for mine. When I looked up, I saw that it belonged to Andy. He pulled me to my feet and as he did, his eyes danced even more in the evening moonlight. We laughed at the way he re-enacted my fall, poking fun at me.

We continued our walk to the cafeteria, and I kept holding onto his hand. I saw a grin slowly grow on his face as he looked down at my soft purple gloves, now wet and cold. I liked the feel of his large hand gripping mine, steadying me as I walked, now more cautiously. He smiled an endearing smile this time. It captured my heart and swept me away. Now, almost fifteen years and three children later; that smile still captures me as I live and work alongside him as his beloved wife.

Andy asked me on our first date on March 22, 1994. I was in my junior year at the Messiah-Philly campus and by then had learned the city well. It was a mild spring that year so he took me downtown to Rittenhouse Square for dinner. Afterwards, we sat high up on the steps of the infamous art museum and looked out over the city's twinkling lights and endless flow of traffic. What I can remember most about that evening was how much we talked. Andy asked questions about my childhood and growing up years and I was open to discussing those things with him. He had heard bits of my testimony at church so some things he had already known. I thought it was wonderful how well he listened and drew me out with each question. He told me that my life story intrigued him.

Throughout that spring, we enjoyed each other's company more and more, and soon became intent in our dating relationship. I even took him to visit the Milton Hershey School because he did not believe that I received an education, clothing, medical and dental care, and a partial college scholarship all free! He met my eighth grade houseparents and we walked through my old student homes. Seeing so many young kids sleeping away from their parents touched Andy's heart and he mentioned how much he would enjoy the possibility of working as a houseparent there one day. It had never crossed my mind to return to

MHS, but I tucked the idea away seriously thinking that perhaps it would be a good fit for me someday.

Dating Andy was refreshing because he was so easy to talk to. He accepted me and my messed up life, without shrinking back or treating me with pity. After awhile, I knew that he was someone that I could trust with my heart. He did not judge me for how I viewed life or for my insecurities. I felt that he was genuinely interested in me. His tenderness and encouragement during those days were priceless.

One summer evening, on the steps of my college dorm on Broad Street, Andy began to tell me about himself, and this small glimpse into his life was something that I have grown to cherish over the years. Andy grew up the fourth of four boys in a western suburb of Chicago called Aurora, Illinois. His oldest brother's name is Thomas Bruce, but he goes by Bruce. The second oldest is named James Eric, who we call Eric and the brother closest in age to Andy is Timothy Paul. Andy was named Andrew Dennis on May 6, 1971.

His mother, Judy Kay Sweetin married Thomas Leon Slamans 46 years ago on February 10, 1962--they are still married today. They raised their four boys in a loving Christian home, but when his father took a second job after

Andy was born, things got even busier for his mother who stayed home until all the boys were school-aged.

Andy grew up like most middle-class suburban boys. He enjoyed the outdoors and played sports in the summer until he was old enough to work. He had his first job at age fourteen, working alongside his brothers and mother at a local grocery store. He saved up enough money to buy his first car when he was fifteen years-old—a 1985 Ford Escort. It was tricked out with a booming stereo, chrome rims, and tinted windows. He drove it even before he had his driver's license. Their family took yearly vacations to places like Colorado for skiing, Florida for the beaches, and everywhere in between.

Active in the church, Andy's parents raised their sons to follow the Lord and to live according to His ways. Andy and his brothers spent a lot of time at church, but during his middle school years, after their family moved across town, Andy decided to follow the influence of his friends. He started attending parties on the weekends and often came home late and drunk. During his high school years, he began experimenting with drugs. Andy knew that his lifestyle went against everything that he had been raised to believe, but he could not refuse his friends or the girls who came calling for him to go out.

One particular evening, when Andy was in high school, he returned home drunk, as usual, and well after his curfew. He heard a voice coming from the back bedroom and followed the sound to the end of the hall. He discovered his mother praying. She was weeping and calling on the name of the Lord for Him to save her son, Andy. Her pleading was urgent. When Andy heard her cries, his knees buckled and his heart broke. He knew that he needed to make a change, but just did not know how to do it in his own strength.

Even though Andy spent a good part of his free time going out, he also made time for the youth group program that was held at his church during the week. His youth pastor was a student at Wheaton College and with the help of the senior pastor, designed a youth program for the kids. Unknown to Andy, his youth pastor had placed his name on his personal prayer list and for three years, just as his mother did, he fervently prayed that Andy would make some changes in his life. In the beginning of his senior year, the prayers over Andy's life were answered in an amazing way.

It happened one hot weekend in August. The church that Andy's family regularly attended held their annual fall event. It was called Lay Witness Weekend. It was a simple, yet effective way of communicating the gospel to those who needed encouragement—and it renewed people's faith. Instead of the pastoral staff designing the services and bringing forth the message, various church members who had a testimony to share about what Jesus was doing, took to the stage.

As the weekend wore on, amazing stories of triumph and victory resonated in the hearts of those who crammed into the hot church each evening. Every time someone shared a testimony, the layers of shame and guilt that had begun to smother Andy's heart were slowly peeled back. He heard the stories that pointed to the Lord's goodness and love, and he was moved to make a decision. It was not one made lightly. On the final night of lay Witness Weekend, Andy decided at last, that he would give his life to Jesus and fully live for Him.

Andy's senior year turned out to be very different from his previous years in school because he talked a lot about Jesus to his friends. He shared the love of Jesus with them and told them how much Jesus had changed his life. His classmates teased him, calling him "Bible Thumper" because he carried his Bible with him everywhere. He changed the friends that he hung out with and even made amends with those he had hurt when he was partying and drinking. After his conversion, he had no desire to party. He did not struggle with wanting to drink, either, but instead surrounded himself with other Christians because they were an encouragement to him. He truly was a different person. As a result, he listened to the Holy Spirit's whisper to go serve the hurting and lost youth in America's cities. His obedience led him to the kids in Philadelphia.

~~~~~~

As we sat on Broad Street that evening we watched the rush-hour traffic dwindle, and our hearts turned from love to grace for one another. We had come to Christ in our own very different ways and neither of us could pretend that there was no residue to work through from our experiences. Nevertheless, what took place that night was a marvelous spiritual awakening for the both of us. We realized that we were two very different people who had found the one thing in common that would stitch our hearts together for eternity—the amazing forgiveness and grace of the Lord Jesus Christ. We gave that grace to one another that evening and have relied on it throughout our marriage ever since.

CHAPTER FIVE

You would not know, seeing how good our marriage is, that our dating months were turbulent, but they were. For starters, I was new at trusting—anyone-- with my heart. After growing up with so much loss and instability, I struggled to believe that Andy would stay around and that he was committed to me. I expected him to lose interest in me after a few months because so many others close to me had gone away. I knew that my friendships did not run deep because of a very personal fear I had of abandonment. I was also afraid of getting close to Andy because the closer we grew, the more I was faced with the decision of how far our relationship would go.

I also had so many emotional issues I was dealing with that I did not feel I had much to offer Andy. I battled insecurity and depression throughout the time that we dated. In fact, as we continued our relationship, Andy noted that I was very "needy" and "clingy". It was difficult to hear and I knew that this emotional need to cling came from so much hurt that I had experienced growing up, but I did not know how to communicate that to him. The last thing that I wished to do was push him away. I longed to meet his needs in the many ways he had met mine, but I did not know how. Over the following months, this became a daily prayer of mine—that I would grow to give Andy all that he was giving to me.

Nine months after we began our dating relationship Andy suggested that we take a break from seeing one another. It was during my senior year at Messiah College and just after the Christmas holiday. Andy had graduated from Eastern College the previous May and he chose to stay in the city to work alongside me and the other youth workers at the church. I had already met his family during his college Graduation and even visited his home in Illinois for a weekend that fall. I thought we were doing well, but Andy felt that he needed the space.

His suggestion to take a break devastated me. Nevertheless, I knew at the time that there were things that I had done to make our relationship difficult. Even though Andy spent a great deal of time and energy encouraging me and reassuring me of his commitment, I continued to battle depression. Looking back on it now, I understand why he needed some time apart. I *was* draining, but I was also very hurt and upset at the thought of us being away from one another.

I called frequently during the first few weeks that Andy was back home in Illinois. He was nice to me on the phone, but I could hear the distance in his voice. I knew that he was pulling away and there was nothing that I could do about it. I continued calling him for a few more weeks, but then I felt the Lord telling me to stop calling and to trust Him for the outcome of our relationship—and that is what I set my heart on doing.

While Andy was away, I focused my energy on finding someone from church to talk to about our break up. I also knew that I needed counseling for myself. I was becoming too engrossed in our relationship and I did not want this separation to do me in. Fortunately, I met a counselor who attended the same church as me. She was an amazing woman who had such an elegance and grace about her. Her love of the Lord was her beauty and I was drawn to her because of it. She counseled me from the Bible and showed me some things in God's word that I had never heard or read before. One particular passage of Scripture that we spent many weeks on is in Jeremiah 17:5-8:

This is what the Lord says, cursed is the one who trusts in man, who depends on flesh for his strength and whose heart turns away from the Lord.

He will be like a bush in the wastelands; he will not see prosperity when it comes. He will dwell in the parched places of the desert, in a salt land where no one lives.

But blessed is the man who trusts in the Lord, whose confidence is in him. He will be like a tree planted by the water that sends out its roots by the stream.

It does not fear when heat comes; its leaves are always green. It has no worries in a year of drought and never fails to bear fruit."

I set my heart on memorizing that portion of scripture and it became my food day and night as I began to work through the many years of loss, rejection, and turmoil. I felt like I was finally *feeling* things, and the wall that I had built around my heart, began falling.

During my childhood, I had lost everything and everyone that mattered to me, but I had not taken the time to process it until that winter while Andy was away. I knew that the road I was beginning to travel—the road to healing--was going to be a long one. That winter, I allowed myself to feel the weight of my pain for the first time in my life, and the freedom that came from it surprised me. As I sought healthy ways of thinking about God, and myself I grew stronger as a young woman. I knew that my past had defined me thus far, but I did not want it to *determine* my future. My confidence in Christ increased because I finally understood that I was special to God and set apart for Him.

I believe that a Christian's journey takes place in stages. When I first came to Christ, initially I looked to Him as my Savior. He saved me from my heartbreak and gave me a safe place to reside in His heart and loving arms. I drew comfort from His Word and from the people that He surrounded me with. I learned in Philadelphia, that I was not alone in my struggles and pain, and that I could even help minister to teens like me *because* of my experiences.

However, as I entered into this very intimate relationship with Andy, I felt that the Lord was asking me to trust *Him* with my heart. It was a deeper level, I was certain of it, and because I loved Andy so much, I felt that I needed to begin this process in order to be healed and made whole. That winter, I knew that even if Andy was not the one for me to marry, I wanted to stand alongside whoever it was to be, as a wife and not as emotional baggage. I did not want to be "needy" or "draining" and I wanted someone who loved me because I had something to offer him in return.

I was not sure how Andy had spent those few months that we were apart, but apparently, God spoke to him a confirmation of our relationship. Later that spring, I received a package at my dorm bearing an Illinois return address and I immediately recognized the handwriting as Andy's. I ripped the package open and in it was a purple (my favorite color) NIKE athletic windbreaker and a simple Happy Birthday card signed *Andy*. I took it as a sign that he was still interested in me.

That May, when I graduated from Messiah College, my aunt, my dad, twin sister, and Andy along with extended family, were there applauding my efforts. Even though my early childhood years were tremendously difficult, that graduation day was another beginning of new dreams for me. I believed that I could be and do anything because the Lord was with me and I knew with all my heart that He loved me and would take care of me—and it felt wonderful putting my confidence in Him!

I spent the summer after I graduated from college preparing for a mission trip that the youth staff from Bethel Temple was organizing. Andy and I, along with five other leaders planned to take our 20 most mature teens to California, Mexico, and Arizona for three weeks. It was the first mission trip for me, and I was excited to be a part of such a wonderful excursion.

While out West, we hiked the falls of Yosemite National Park and camped inside the park a few nights. We also swam and played on California's beaches and spent a week at a Christian camp playing in the lakes and cabins on their immense campground. Many of our teens had not seen nature this wonderful--having lived in Philadelphia their entire lives. They were delighted to experience such beauty and magnificent scenery.

While in Mexico, we poured a cement foundation for a small church that was being built, and ran a kids' day camp for the children who lived and ate at the garbage dumps in Tijuana. The poverty in Mexico was fierce and our teens from North Philadelphia counted their blessings because of how much they discovered they truly had back home.

In the evenings, we built campfires and touched base with the youth about all that they were seeing and experiencing. Intimacy is easier in the flickering firelight and the kids talked frankly about the joys and concerns that they were having. We challenged them to a new way of thinking about Christ by way of serving Him and they learned His merciful heart as we worked among the poor and outcast. Some had previously made decisions to follow Him and the ones who did accept Christ wanted to go deeper. The mission trip proved to be the perfect venue.

My favorite memory took place on June 29, 1995—about a week and a half into the mission trip. We were at a Christian camp located in northern California on the beautiful Hume Lake. The snow-capped mountains were visible in the distance and the camp's grounds were enormous. That week there were over thirty different youth groups and their counselors, from all over the country, on the premises—over seven hundred of us in all!

On that particular morning, I helped lead devotions for our teen girls in my cabin. I had grown to love hanging out with these young ladies all along the trip. This was part of our daily routine prior to heading to the large cafeteria for breakfast. We usually met Andy and the group of guys from his cabin on the pathway, but Andy was not with the group that morning. When we got to breakfast he was nowhere around. I thought it was odd, but I did not spend too much time worrying about him because the other leaders in his cabin assured me that he just decided to skip breakfast. I spent the rest of the morning running my activities as usual wondering in the back of my mind where Andy could be.

When it was time to meet for lunch, he was waiting at the table with his group, but he barely gave me a nod. When I tried to start a conversation with him, he was distant and quiet. My heart went into my throat because I did not understand his mood. I went through my memory bank of the previous day trying to remember if I had said or done anything to offend him. I came up with nothing.

I ate lunch with the girls while I silently wondered what was bothering Andy. After lunch, we had scheduled free time, so Andy approached me and asked if I wanted to take a raft out onto the lake. I agreed, of course, because I thought it would be a good opportunity for us to talk and catch up. We headed to the boys' cabin deep in the woods to fetch the inflatable raft and we carried it down to the water's edge.

Once in the water, I felt my heart grow calm as I watched Andy use his long strong arms to paddle us deep into the center of the lake. I helped him move the raft forward using my arms, as I lay on my stomach. After creating quite a distance from the rest of the campers who were splashing in canoes and jumping off the edges of their rafts into the cold water, Andy and I rolled over onto our backs and stared up at the white puffy clouds passing over us. The raft bobbed up and down lulling us to sleep.

I gazed at the snow-capped mountains in the distance and loved God's magnificent creation. I heard Andy sigh as he lay next to me and I began to speak, but then he spoke at the same time. I stopped abruptly waiting for him to finish.

There was an awkward silence and then he asked me what I would say if he asked me to marry him. He had asked this question of me before, and I always said the same thing: *I would say yes, **if** you asked me... Are you **asking** me?* He would always say, *No, I was just wondering what you would say*. Then I would laugh at him.

There on the lake, I said the same thing. I told him that I would say yes...*if he asked me*. Then, smiling, I asked him if he was asking me! This time he met my gaze and then began to untie the string that was holding his swim trunks in place. He pulled out a delicate looking gold ring with a marquis diamond in the center and a row of four smaller diamonds that ran down each side of the ring. I could not believe he tied my engagement ring to his swim trunks! *Love makes you do strange things,* I thought.

Time stood still as I looked around at the sparkling lake, mountains, and woods that surrounded the camp property and I knew that Andy had picked the most beautiful place to ask for my hand in marriage. He asked me, Deanna Rosetta Bradley, if I would become his wife! I said yes and we hugged and kissed. Andy led us in prayer for our future together. It felt good to be wanted. Before that day, I had a difficult time believing that anyone could desire me or want to be with me—especially because of all the problems I had grown up with. Now, Andy and I were committed to each other for a lifetime. It was an awesome feeling. I had never received reassurance like this growing up. This acceptance was what had been missing in my life for so many years.

We lay on the raft some more enjoying the warm sun on our backs. Thinking about the events of the day, I decided to ask him if this was why he had missed breakfast that morning. He told me that he was up early so that he could fast and pray one last time. He wanted to be certain God would give me to him as his wife. He also told me that his time away in Illinois the past winter was spent praying about that very thing. I was stunned. It had never dawned on me that he would spend that time away because he desired to be *closer* to me.

As we paddled back to the lake's shore, some of the kids from our youth group came up alongside us in their large canoes. They asked to switch our raft for their canoe so Andy and I agreed. When I stepped into the canoe, the bottom of it was filled with red, long-stemmed roses. I looked up at Andy and he told me that the flowers were for me. I scooped up as many as I could in my arms, grinning the whole time at how he had tricked me. We passed other groups of kids in canoes and as we got closer, they stood, leaned over, and laid more roses into my already full arms. I was in complete shock at this point.

Andy led the canoe to the edge of the lakeshore so that I could climb out. It proved to be a difficult maneuver with an armload of roses, but he steadied me as I made the climb. Then he paddled the canoe to the inlet for storage while I waited for him along the shore. As I did, campers from all over the complex approached me with a single long-stemmed rose in their hands. One by one they each gave me a rose and told me congratulations. I did not know many of the kids. These campers were from all over the country! I smiled and accepted their gift as I began to realize that the entire campground knew about this engagement! The amount of roses that I received was so large that I needed a 5-gallon bucket to carry them. We filled the bucket with water and Andy helped me carry it to my cabin.

When we entered the cabin, I saw that the girls had placed rose petals on my bed and all over the bathroom sink and tub. They had decorated it beautifully! The mirror had writing on it in lipstick that read, *Congratulations, Andy & Deanna!* I was deeply touched by their joyous spirits as they joined in our engagement celebration! I cried tears of joy for this church family of young women that I had grown to love over the past two years.

That evening, Andy and I did not eat dinner in the cafeteria with the rest of the campers. Instead, we enjoyed a quiet, romantic meal at a restaurant on the grounds usually reserved for private groups. We caught our breath from the rush of the day and then went about the business of setting the wedding date. We chose the Saturday after Thanksgiving--November 25 of that same year. We knew that both of our families would have time around Thanksgiving to join us for our wedding.

The mission trip was capped off with an overnight stay in one of the most beautiful places in America—the Grand Canyon. Some of our youth workers and a few of the teenage boys hiked down to the bottom of the canyon and back up in one day—Andy was part of that daring group. Even though they were advised by the park ranger not to attempt it because of the heat, it did not deter them. They carried several one-gallon jugs of water and walking sticks, and made the round trip before sundown. Exhausted, they were the first ones asleep that evening.

~~~~~~

It was a mild day for the Saturday after Thanksgiving-- our wedding day—November 25, 1995. We scheduled the ceremony for later that evening. As a bride, preparing for her moment of a lifetime, I reflected on the past seven years as a Christian. I knew that everything was coming together nicely. I was finally allowing God to bind my wounded heart and I truly believed that He was remaking me into someone new and different.

When I walked down the aisle, with my father at my side, I could not believe how much had changed since I was a little girl. Both of my sisters were my bridesmaids along with some wonderful girlfriends. My maid of honor was also a strong mentor to me, and someone that I tremendously adored. My aunt, who took us in years earlier after the death of our mother and grandmother, stood in as the Mother-of-the-Bride. Family from both my mom and dad's side were there along with the closest friends Andy and I had ever known. They surrounded us as we made our undying commitment to one another.

I had made it through a lonesome childhood because the Lord placed in my life so many truly, wonderful and Godly people. That day He set me, a lonely girl, in a family.

Part Two

"The Lord is close to the broken hearted and saves those who are crushed in spirit..." --Psalm 34:18

CHAPTER SIX

In Job 1:9-12 Satan inquires of the Lord the state of Job's heart. He has the audacity to *accuse* God of protecting Job from calamity and argues that it is for this reason alone that Job has remained faithful to the Lord all these years. *"Why shouldn't he respect you?"* Satan *remarked. "You are like a wall protecting not only him, but his entire family and all his property. You make him successful in whatever he does and his flocks and herds are everywhere. Try taking away everything he owns and he will curse you to your face."*

The Lord replied, "All right, Satan, do what you want with anything that belongs to him, but don't harm Job." Then Satan left.

I have always been fascinated with this exchange between God and Satan. For some unknown reason, the Lord allows us this rare opportunity to eavesdrop on a conversation that He is having in the heavenlies. So many times we think we know the reasons for someone else's sufferings—we often make false assumptions about God when we buy in to the line of thinking that says perhaps it is the person's lack of faith, spiritual immaturity, or maybe even God's wrath that this calamity has befallen them. However, we rarely think of God giving Satan *permission* to strike us with his deathblows.

The Lord Jesus had a similar conversation with Satan regarding the fate of Simon Peter. Prior to the Lord's death and resurrection heaven touched earth, when Jesus revealed to a man the dialogue that must have taken place between Himself and Satan. As humans, we lack the privilege of knowing what the spiritual forces are doing. Jesus told Peter: *"Satan has asked to sift you as wheat. But I have prayed for you, Simon that your faith may not fail. And when you have turned back, strengthen your brothers."—Luke 22:31*

The answers to the questions of why the Lord gives us opportunities to be tested are His to know. If we are not careful, we can become tempted to believe what our brokenness speaks to us: *Doesn't God love me? Why would He allow this horrendous thing to take place? Aren't I a good enough Christian to avoid this type of suffering?*

Even Christ's disciples assumed that a man born blind was deserving of such a condition. They asked him, *"Rabbi, who sinned, this man, or his parents, that he was born blind?"*

*"Neither this man nor his parents sinned," said Jesus, "but this happened so that **the work of God** might be displayed in his life. As long as it is day, we must do the work of him who sent me. Night is coming, when no one can work. While I am in the world, I am the light of the world."*—John 9:1-5.

We presume that our sufferings are about us but God testifies repeatedly in His Word of the glory that He seeks from changing lives and making all things new. The book of Isaiah speaks of the Lord's desire to bring his people out of captivity so that **His** name will be great. The Lord even shows Moses the purposes of Pharaoh's hardened heart in Exodus 11:9, when He tells him *"Pharaoh will refuse to listen to you—**so that my wonders may be multiplied** in Egypt."*

A few chapters earlier, Moses tried to use his limitations as a reason for his reluctance to speak to Pharaoh. He told God that he was not an eloquent speaker and had a slow tongue. God resented Moses' remark and answered him, *"Who gave man his mouth? Who makes him deaf or dumb? Who gives him sight or makes him blind? Is it not I, the Lord?"*—Exodus 4:10-12

In other words, our limitations, tests, blunders, and stumbles are how God gets our attention and how He works in this fallen world. He knows we fall short, and that is okay. He shows us these revelations in Scripture as a source of comfort when we are stunned by life's unpredictable occurrences. I am strongly convinced of this comfort and now know it very well. However, I have not always seen God's handiwork in my life in this way. In fact, I spent some years offended with the way God chose to do things and it cost me dearly.

~~~~~~

I learned this deeper truth about God's glorification amidst our suffering only after I had my three children, Kobe, Korri, & AJ. Our firstborn son, Kobe was born at 24 weeks gestation—which is only about 5 ½ months along in the pregnancy. A normal pregnancy should run close to 40 weeks. I was nowhere near that when I went into labor with him. Andy and I had been married three years when we discovered, that while carrying Kobe, I had an incompetent cervix. This means I cannot hold a baby in the womb for very long without medical intervention. The muscles of my cervix are not strong and begin to dilate after the baby puts on a significant amount of weight during the second trimester.

I was 22 weeks along and out in the Chicago area with Andy visiting his family over the Christmas holiday. On

December 29, 1998, I went into the after-hours hospital clinic because I thought my water broke; and after a thorough examination, the on-call gynecologist informed me that I was already dilated 3cm and that my cervix was thinned and effaced—but my water bag was still intact. He asked me if I noticed any contractions over the past few days. I had not so this news was very alarming to both Andy and I. The doctor then told us that my body had already started the labor process and that the baby could not survive if he was born this early. The lungs on an infant this small are just beginning to grow, if they exist at all.

While Andy and I were trying to get over the initial shock of what was happening, the doctor prepared me for a surgical procedure called a *cervical cerclage*. He planned to tie what was left of the cervical tissue closed as much as he could to prevent the baby from "slipping" out. There was not much of the cervical tissue to work with at this point, he informed us, but he assured us that he would do his best to tighten it. He also gave me medicine to relax the uterus so that I would not have anymore "silent" contractions.

After the surgery, the doctor wanted to send me home. I asked, instead, to be taken to a hospital that was equipped to care for preemie babies. The doctor agreed and I was driven by ambulance to the University of Illinois-Chicago Medical Center or UIC located in the city near the "loop" close to downtown Chicago. It is a Level 3 hospital able to care for the smallest of infants. I was admitted on an emergency basis, with the goal of finishing out the 16 remaining weeks of my pregnancy there on bed rest. Because this seemed so far away, I set my sights on keeping the pregnancy viable day by day, while we began the long fight for our unborn baby's life.

During the two weeks that followed, Andy and I prayed fervently for our baby. Through the many ultrasounds, we learned that it was a boy and began finalizing the list of names that we were thinking about giving him after he was born. Andy stayed with me every night that I was in the hospital, only returning to his parents' home in Aurora every few days for a shower and to update his parents on my condition. When he was not by my side, he was just a phone call and an hour drive away. At one point, my two sisters flew in from the east coast to be with me. I was deeply touched by their kindness as they chatted with me, braided my hair and gave me a manicure and pedicure. These loving acts helped keep my mind off of what I thought was an impossible situation.

Andy and I could not help but think that the reason this was happening was because there was something wrong with the baby; but surprisingly, every ultrasound indicated a healthy boy who measured slightly larger than his gestational age. We were told that if I carried as far as 24 weeks, there was a higher percentage of survival—a 60 percent chance. This seemed attainable and so we prayed some more that the Lord would be merciful and allow our son to make it to the point of "life". I received a daily dose of steroid shots, which through my bloodstream, would enter the placenta and speed the growth of our tiny baby boy. His lungs were where the medical staff focused their concern. Without strong lungs, he could not live on his own.

On the morning I reached 24 weeks, I had a little party for myself in the hospital room. It was a prayer of thanksgiving to the Lord for helping us to make it this far in the pregnancy. Exactly one day later, however, my water bag became too heavy for my cervix and the contractions began again. Only this time they were not "silent"—I felt them strong. The nurses monitored them and discovered that they were coming too close together. I had already been on the muscle relaxant for two weeks and was using the strongest dose possible. The doctors tried everything possible to slow the contractions, but after many examinations and discussions, it was necessary that I deliver the baby that night.

The activity in the room became frantic as fear gripped my heart. I knew that it was too soon to deliver this baby, so I silently prayed again while I breathed through each contraction when they hit. Because Kobe was laying breech in the womb, I was hurriedly prepared for a c-section. I would not be able to deliver him naturally because his tiny head could get stuck. As I lie there with my legs numb in the operating room, I could hear his tiny heart beat on the monitor. Andy stood at my head and there was a curtain up so that I could not see what was taking place. In order not to panic, I began to count my blessings as the doctor made her first cut across my abdomen.

I spoke softly with Andy during the surgery and tried to enjoy the moment even though it was traumatic and not at all how I envisioned the birth of my firstborn. Nevertheless, Kobe Slamans was born at 11:00 pm on January 12, 1999. It did not pay much attention to the date at the time, but several months later it dawned on me that Kobe was born on the *exact day that my mom died 18 years earlier.*

I peeked at our little boy before the nurses rushed him into the NICU. He weighed 1 lb. and 12 ounces and was 33cm, or 13 inches long. By the time that Kobe was born, Andy's parents, two brothers and their wives were already at the hospital. They tried to get a look at our baby in the NICU but the situation was distressing, so they were not able to enter or see him because of the many doctors and nurses that surrounded him. In the meantime, I was in the recovery room waiting to get some feeling back into my legs and feet.

After an hour, the nurse wheeled my bed into the NICU so that I could see my new baby boy. He looked even more helpless and fragile than I imagined hooked up to so many wires and machines. My heart broke because I feared the worst—that I would lose him. Andy and I were told that one of his lungs had already collapsed and because he did not have the surfactant lining developed in them, it was impossible to inflate the lung again, so he was living on one lung. His heart rate, blood oxygen level and vital signs were looking good for an infant this tiny, but the nurses wanted to see them remain stable for another few more hours.

I touched Kobe's tiny chest with my hand and spoke to him for the first time. I saw him react to the sound of my voice and realized that he had heard it before as I carried him right underneath my beating heart. I longed to hold him, but knew that I could not—at least not yet. I would have to wait for that moment when he grew stronger. Andy helped the nurse wheel my bed into the labor and delivery room. All we could do was wait. As we waited, we prayed some more for the Lord to help Kobe survive. We asked for a miracle and we asked for His sovereign will to be done. We talked of how cute Kobe was--and the fact that he was born alive. God had answered so many prayers so far.

I tried to sleep but it eluded me. Andy checked on Kobe every so often and spoke with his parents and brothers as they stood around waiting for the latest report. At 2 a.m., his family headed home and 2 hours later Kobe's doctor told us that he was no longer alive.

He died at 4 a.m. on January 13, 1999.

It was the saddest day of my life.

A little while later, the doctor brought Kobe in to our room in a small wicker basket. He was dressed in white preemie clothes and had a white hat on his head. His face was bruised from the tiny oxygen tubes that were taped to him and inserted in his nostrils. His arms and legs were so skinny. I held the basket to my chest and stared into his little face, but felt nothing because of the shock. I could not take in all that was happening because the loss was too great.

The three days that followed were a blur. I had to begin the business of recovering from a c-section, which, under normal circumstances, usually takes second place to the business of caring for a newborn. For me, however, the pain that existed in my abdomen matched what was in my heart. I could not believe that my first child was gone! Sadness enveloped Andy and I as we met with doctors and nurses about our son, my staples, stitches, and the level of my pain.

We decided to have Kobe's body autopsied so that the doctor's could learn all that they could about what may have caused this early delivery. The morning after Kobe died, I noticed on the desk beside my bed a lavender box. In it contained Kobe's hat, clothes, and a card with his hand and footprints. A tiny lock of his hair was clipped and taped to another card, and his hospital ankle bracelet was inside the box as well. I was grateful for this loving act of kindness from the hospital staff. It then dawned on me how often this must take place at a hospital like this. Caring for the smallest of babies must be a wondrous, yet frustrating task—especially when things go wrong. I was immensely appreciative of all that was done for my baby boy.

Interestingly enough, the two weeks that I stayed off my feet was enough to cause atrophy in my leg muscles and create even more discomfort for me when I started walking again. The day before I was discharged, I wrenched my back or hip, while getting dressed and the pain radiated down my entire right leg. It did not let up no matter what I did. I used ice, heat, and tried to stretch it out but it only grew worse. By the time I was supposed to leave the hospital, I could barely walk. This only added to my heartbreak.

The next day, with prescriptions for pain and a dressing over my incision, I prepared to leave the hospital that I had entered over two weeks earlier. I was not ready to go, but there was no longer any reason for me to stay. It was January 15 when Andy pushed me in a wheelchair down the smooth quiet hallways toward the hospital exit. Our loneliness and sorrow were heavy. I held the lavender box on my lap and cried silently. I told Andy that there was supposed to be three of us leaving the hospital—not two. He nodded, said "I know…" and he cried along with me.

The Lord tells us in Psalm 34:18 that He is *close to the brokenhearted and saves those who are crushed in spirit.* During those long days that I spent recovering, it did not feel like the Lord was close to me, but that did not mean that He was not. In fact, I believe that the reason that I am able to write about this as part of my story of hope is that He was very close to me even many years after Kobe died. However, in those early years I grieved as if I had no hope.

I spent the remaining six weeks recovering at Andy's parents' home in Aurora, Illinois. It was necessary to follow up my care with the doctors who had treated Kobe and me. I was glad to still be in Illinois because I was not ready to return to our home in Philadelphia. Going home would mean getting on with the business of living without our son and I was not ready for what all that entailed.

Days and nights ran together as time lingered further and further away from the day that I gazed upon my son's face. I felt that a cruel joke was being played on me the day that my milk came in and there was no baby to feed. I wept one day in the shower as the drops fell down the drain. I did most of my crying in the shower because I could watch my milk drip and marvel, even in my grief, at the complex body that the Lord had given me.

I also watched Andy closely during those early days after Kobe died and saw his prayer life become more vibrant. He spent long moments in solitude praying and seeking the Lord's face. He had been confronted with a Holy and Magnificent God whose Sovereignty had spoken. The decision was final over Kobe's life. He was gone and there was nothing that Andy could do about it. He did not hold God responsible for this loss. He accepted--it even though it was the most difficult thing that he ever had to do.

My reaction to the Lord's mighty hand that gives and takes away was much different. I did not seek God's face. I could not enter into fellowship with the Lord when my heart was so broken. It was too painful to acknowledge the choice that He had made over our son's life. Even when I had asked Him out of the depths of my soul, He answered "no" and I could not understand why. I felt the wound that was barely healed from my childhood begin to open up again. This time it ran deep and I feared that I would drown in it. After all, I had already experienced the loss of my mother and grandmother within months of each other 18 years ago. My childhood was a fragmented memory of dashed hopes and broken dreams. Now, on top of everything else, the one thing that I thought I could have for myself, my baby boy, was taken away as well. I was at a loss for words.

When Andy and I returned to Philadelphia, I was still dealing with the sharp pain in my hip and back. The painkillers that I had been on were running low and I needed to find a longer-term solution for healing the pinched nerve that was plaguing me. I decided to go to a chiropractor and he helped to ease the pain quite a bit. Still, after long days working at the private school where I was the Administrative Assistant, the pain could shoot down my leg unexpectedly and debilitate me once again.

One evening while stretching out my lower back, I was reminded of the story of Jacob wrestling with God at Peniel. In Genesis 32:24-31 we see that Jacob was alone and he wrestled a man until daybreak. Because the man could not overpower Jacob, he touched his hip socket as he continued to wrestle him. Then at daybreak, when the man says that he must go, Jacob tells him that he will not let him go until he receives a blessing. The man, or in fact, the Lord, as we discover later, changes Jacob's name to Israel and then blesses him. Jacob goes away from Peniel with a blessing and a limp in his gait because of his wrenched hip.

While I stretched, I cried because I needed to hear from God that through all of this turmoil He in fact did bless me through the loss of our son. I knew in my spirit that I was still wrestling with God over the decision that He made concerning Kobe. I struggled with reading His word and I had no desire to pray. Whenever I listened to the pastor at church preach about God's promises, my heart grew cold and I felt sarcasm rise up in my spirit. But that night, when the Lord reminded me of Jacob, I asked for a blessing. I wept and prayed to the Lord because I hoped that through time, this tragedy would one day bless me—even if I was left forever with a sore hip.

A few weeks later, I contacted the pastor of Bethel Temple Church and asked to see him and the elders for prayer. I told Andy that it was my desire to be healed. I had taken the promise of healing found in James 5:13-15 for myself:

"Is any one of you in trouble? He should pray. Is anyone happy? Let him sing songs of praise. Is any one of you sick? He should call the elders of the church to pray over him and anoint him with oil in the name of the Lord. And the prayer offered in faith will make the sick person well; the Lord will raise him up."

Andy joined me in an upper room of the church as the elders and pastor surrounded me in prayer. My head was anointed with oil and I cried for my sore hip and my broken heart. I knew that I was sick and I was fearful that I would not find my way back to God again if I remained in this state. My trust in Him was shaken when Kobe died. I discovered that afternoon during prayer that my trust had been built on my circumstances and not on the foundation of God Himself. I was the man in scripture who had built his house upon the sand and when the winds and waves came, my house came down with a violent crash. Thankfully, many were praying for me, even before that day; and those prayers are what brought me healing.

CHAPTER SEVEN

The year following Kobe's death was a difficult one. I was not prepared for some people's reactions to our situation. Many did not know what to say to Andy and me regarding our tragic circumstance. We found out quickly though, that there was nothing that people *could* say that would ease our pain. This is often the case with loss. Many asked us questions about our ability to get pregnant again. In fact, it put some people's minds at ease when we report that *yes, we could have another baby*—if we wanted one. But, I did not even want to think about another pregnancy with my sore back and the traumatic turn of events that still plagued my waking and sleeping hours.

Other well-intentioned friends and family felt the need to remind us that Kobe was in a "better" place. I felt selfish thinking that I wanted him here with me, not in Heaven. I also began to resent the care-free pregnancies that my friends and family enjoyed. Their babies entered the world leaving on their mothers only stretch marks and soreness. It was too much for me to celebrate their happiness when deep down I was still suffering.

When my back had healed somewhat, Andy and I spent our free time in our Philadelphia row home completing the renovations that we had begun on the house over one year before. It was a large house, by row home standards. There were three floors (not counting the basement), five bedrooms and one bathroom. Because we had so much space, we had decided the year before, to rent out some of the rooms to college students who attended Temple University.

With no baby to care for, I continued my work at a private school close to the Fairmount section of the city. The Philadelphia Mennonite High School was where I was the Administrative Assistant. Before the pregnancy, I had also taken on teaching a drama/theatre class so that the students could work on some performances for the holiday season. Andy reluctantly continued his youth ministry position at Bethel Temple church in the evenings and on the weekends. We were both so deeply affected by this sudden loss, that getting back to our normal routines did not seem right—or fair.

Prior to getting pregnant, Andy and I had begun the discussion he started years ago about the possibility of working as houseparents at MHS. In fact, we had already submitted our applications for the Full-Time Houseparent positions even before Kobe was born. We were waiting for a reply from the school when the complicated events surrounding the pregnancy took place, and had even received several calls to schedule an on-campus interview while we were out in the Chicago area.

At the time, we kindly explained that we would not be available for an interview anytime soon and that the next few months were critical to our pregnancy. We asked the school to keep our applications on file for a later date; and in April of 1999--almost four months after losing Kobe; we contacted the school and decided to visit the campus for the two-day interview.

On the evening before the interview, in the student home's guest apartment, I could not help but reflect on my time at the school, and I was reminded again why we were choosing to become houseparents. While Andy and I talked about the upcoming interview, I thought of the fond memories that I had experienced when I lived on that beautiful campus.

Andy also shared with me his desire to be God's instrument in the lives of kids who did not have all that he had growing up. He also shared with me a dream that he once had when he was a little boy. He dreamed of owning a large house and having it filled with kids—but they were not his kids. There were maybe 10-15 young kids living with him, and he, along with his wife, helped to raise these children that were not his own.

That night, we also talked of a family in Philadelphia that we had grown to adore. They lived close to us in our neighborhood and had made a lasting impression on Andy and me. They were the Cuffie children and their family consisted of a single mother and her four kids. The oldest boy was named Calvin Cuffie, who we called Webster, the second boy was Daultry, the third boy's name was Jerome and their youngest sister was named Athenia, who went by Kat Kat. They were beautiful, kind-hearted children, like their mother, Michelle, and if Andy and I had room in our car when we passed by their house, we would often take them for a day with us.

The things we did with the Cuffie's were numerous: we played games, watched movies, ate popcorn, had sleepovers, went to the fireworks, rode bikes, and we fed them—a lot. Four kids can drain the food supply but we did not mind because we loved being with them. After awhile, we began taking them to church. They became a regular presence at youth group outings and events. The time spent with this family was priceless. They were, in a sense, the first kids that we ever "house-parented."

I had doubts that I would make a good housemother because I had grown up with no family structure worth speaking of. *How could I raise a "family" of kids who were not even mine?* I thought as I ironed my clothes for the next morning's interview. Then I felt the Lord reassure me by saying, *If you love the kids that I give you in your student home the way that you have loved the Cuffies this past year, then I know you* will *be a good housemother.* Despite my misgivings, the interview went extremely well and we received the offer for the job.

As we made the drive home to Philly, we prayed about making a move to Hershey. We sought the Lord to show us why He placed this desire on our hearts and the fact that He even opened the door for us to step through. We wondered if we could work together as a couple. After various confirmations in our spirit, we began our career at the Milton Hershey School on November 1, 1999; almost one year after our son was born. I was still deeply affected by his death but moving to another place and starting a new career was something that I was definitely looking forward to.

Houseparenting proved to be an instant challenge because right away we became "parents" of twelve teenage boys. They were a lot of fun to be around, but the work kept us extremely busy. The first students we ever had resided at Student Home Switzerland. Their ages ranged from 13 to 18 years-old. The houseparent job demands a split-shift schedule. Our day began with an early morning wake-up and chore time followed by breakfast with the students prior to getting them off to school. Then we had six hours off during the morning and early afternoon hours, followed by time working again with the students when they returned from school until bedtime. Sometimes work occurred even in the middle of the night--especially if students were ill or mischievous.

We thoroughly enjoyed the job because it allowed us to spend time together as a couple. We also enjoyed attending our students' plays, concerts, and sporting events. We spent the weekends on-duty relaxing by taking the guys shopping or to the movies. Andy was always ready to play basketball with anyone who was around, and with a lot of teenage boys around, he was able to play lots of quick pick-up games!

On Kobe's one-year birthday, I told Andy that I wanted to take the evening off. I needed to use that precious time to honor our son. I bought scrapbook materials and read my pregnancy journal for about the twentieth time. It truly was a sad day, but I did not mind because I *wanted* to feel sad— for him. I spent the day and evening designing a scrapbook.

It was emotional, but I needed to do this for my own closure.

Later that night, Andy bought me a small, round chocolate birthday cake with a number 1 candle on top. We sang "Happy Birthday" to Kobe and cried. Even though the pain was intense, I felt strangely comforted by it. It told me that *he mattered* to us—even one year later.

That weekend, when we went off-duty, we returned to our row home in Philadelphia. We were living in it, somewhat, on a temporary basis during our early months at MHS. We still wanted to spend a lot of our time off in Philadelphia because we missed visiting with friends and attending church. We had developed many friendships over the years so we tried to keep in touch as much as possible.

That Saturday night, prior to preparing for church in the morning, I climbed the stairs to the third story bedroom that accessed the lower of the two roofs on the house. Then, with Andy's help, I climbed to the higher roof and sat down. Andy joined me a few seconds later and we sat together on the rooftop and gazed at the city's skyline. Stars are difficult to see in the city, especially around the campus of Temple University. Streetlights and mild traffic are what encompass the noise of city life at night. I was grateful for the solitude because the evening was meant for us to talk and take in the view.

After a few minutes, I sent off a single, foil, helium balloon that was in the shape of a heart. I had purchased it earlier at a card store for Kobe. It read *I Love You from the Bottom of My Heart*. I learned about this simple way to celebrate/grieve a loved one's birthday in a book that I was reading about early infant loss.

As we watched the balloon fade from sight, I was surprised that Andy and I had made it through the first year without our son. Statistically, a marriage has a high percentage of divorce after the death of a child. But, with the Lord's help, Andy had nurtured me through the loss and gently consoled my broken heart. I could not have made it without him. The Lord had given me the perfect husband who knew what I needed most. I knew that evening, that he was the perfect man for me and I was so blessed to have him.

After Kobe's first birthday, we talked quite a bit about trying to have another baby. I was anxious because I still did not understand what it meant to have an incompetent cervix. I feared that we would get pregnant only to lose another child—and I could not go through the same trauma again.

In April of that year, I went to see a specialist at the Hershey Medical Center. The neonatal area of the hospital was also Level 3 and focused its care on the smallest of babies. I was introduced to Dr. John J. Botti, who specialized in infant death and neonatal infections. I hoped that this doctor would understand our needs and, more importantly, my grief.

I met with Dr. Botti, and learned that he was part of a team of high-risk pregnancy doctors who would follow me closely through any of my subsequent pregnancies. I also learned that the cervical cerclage that I received in Illinois is the same procedure that I would need for any of my pregnancies that lasted beyond three months. A stitch would be placed at the neck of the cervix, which is the base of the womb, between thirteen and fourteen weeks' gestation. During the second and third trimester weeks, I would have to carry the baby while on bed rest. The doctor would remove the stitch sometime between thirty-six and thirty-seven weeks, which are the beginning weeks of full-term for a pregnancy.

I liked Dr. Botti because he had a gentle manner and was very matter-of-fact about the details surrounding my previous pregnancy. He explained to me the risks for the procedure but also let me know that he and his team were confident in its success, because they had performed it many times. He noticed the apprehension in my voice as I asked questions and sought clarification. He knew that I wanted a 100 percent guarantee that things would go better the next time around, but he could not give it. High-risk pregnancies are difficult to predict. Only time and prayer would get Andy and me through the next pregnancy.

We spent several months praying about getting pregnant. My prayers were cautious because I was afraid to hope again. I let Andy do most of the praying while I secretly wished that my body was designed differently. Ironically, it took us almost another year to get pregnant. The emotional toll of carrying another child loomed in the backs of our minds, and perhaps this stress had an affect on our fertility. I also wrestled with guilt about having another baby after Kobe. Even though I wanted another child, I did not want to dishonor his memory by concentrating so soon on getting pregnant.

Nevertheless, I did get pregnant in January of 2001, and after the pregnancy was confirmed and I made it through the first trimester, I was given the cervical cerclage that April. I began my pregnancy bed rest at home immediately after the surgery. My due date was October 21 *if* I carried that long. I hoped my body would hold out for six more months.

Voice of Truth[2] is a song released by the Christian music group "Casting Crowns". I love the words because they capture what was in my heart during the next four and a half months that I carried our daughter Korri on bed rest.

Oh, what I would do to have

The kind of faith it takes to step out of this boat I'm in…

Onto the crashing waves

To step out of my comfort zone,

Into the realm of the unknown where Jesus is…

And He's holding out His hand.

But the waves are calling out my name and they laugh at me!

Reminding me of all the times, I've tried before and failed….

The waves, they keep on telling me time and time again…

Boy, you'll never win…you'll never win!

But the Voice of Truth, tells me a different story!

The Voice of Truth says "Do Not Be Afraid,"

And The Voice of Truth says "This is for My glory!"

Out of all the voices calling out to me…

I will choose to listen and believe the Voice of Truth!

I know now how my difficult pregnancies have been used for God's glory, but at the time I could not appreciate any of what He had planned for me. Instead, I struggled enormously with fear while carrying our only daughter. It was so debilitating that it became a stronghold for me. I would wake up in the morning feeling secure about my pregnancy and within a few hours, doubt would creep in and tear down the wall of confidence that I was standing behind.

I could not feel God's love for me because I was so afraid of another death. I cried often and felt that my bed rest would end in vain. Then I would read God's word and search frantically for a thread of truth to hold onto. I wanted to believe God loved me—even though the pain in my heart felt otherwise. I did not want to base my trust in Him on my circumstances, but I failed miserably because all I could see was Kobe's face and his young life that had so quickly slipped away. I often dreamed of having another baby to bury and would wake up startle checking for any sign of movement inside my expanding belly.

I doubted daily whether the pregnancy would last. With the stitch around my cervix, my uterus became highly sensitive and I felt contractions often. The doctors warned me that my body may try to reject the foreign substance—which is one of the risks of having the procedure done. I noticed that if I sat up or got up too much, my contractions would increase, but I grew weary lying on my side day after day. The pain in my hip and back returned reminding me of the road I had traveled a few years before; and the wrestling in my heart returned while my thoughts taunted me.

I was very depressed and nearly drove Andy mad with my tears and worries. He struggled with comforting me because he was dealing with his own anxieties about the pregnancy. He was also running the student home without my help. While I tried to be positive it was difficult because I knew that my body was the enemy against my biggest hope—that I could carry a baby to full-term. I prayed what I felt were hopeless prayers but could do nothing else but wait.

While I spent my waking hours on our living room sofa, many of my friends came to visit and their company took my mind off my worries. Fellow houseparents and the students who lived with me were good companions to my loneliness. Other people who had learned about our previous failed pregnancy began praying that the baby and I would make it to full-term. Our families kept us hopeful with their calls and visits. Their encouragement was what Andy and I needed. Andy spent almost all of his free time with me, and fortunately, the school found someone to assist him with running the student home. We were glad for the help because he did not have to do everything by himself.

After two months on bed rest, summer vacation came and our student home was officially "closed" for six weeks. Our family from out of town came to see us, because I was not permitted to travel, and the time went by faster than usual. I did a lot of my sitting in a lounge chair outside since I longed to have a change in scenery.

Throughout that spring and summer, my doctor visits went well and the baby was developing fine. The beginning of July marked the 24th week of the pregnancy and even though this was a small victory for us, I struggled with the temptation to worry by replaying in my mind all that had happened with Kobe during that time a few years earlier. My emotions were raw because fear still ruled my fragile heart. Somehow, though, through God's kindness, the days and nights grew rhythmic and the haunting memories faded as my belly swelled along with my fingers and toes.

At thirty-one weeks' gestation, I went in for a scheduled doctor's visit. Routinely, my blood pressure was taken, a urine sample was tested and I answered general questions regarding any new symptoms and the frequency of my contractions, etc. That particular day the nurse returned to the room to inform me that there was a trace of protein in my urine. She also noted that my blood pressure was elevated. *I had not experienced a stressful situation that would have given a reason for my blood pressure to rise*, I told her (besides the fact that the entire bed rest event was extremely stressful…but after sixteen weeks, I could not claim that as a defense).

Then Dr. Anthony Ambrose, came in to speak to us. He was another member of the high-risk pregnancy team. We had met him before during checkups so the fact that he came in to see me was part of the routine. After reviewing with us my urine analysis and blood pressure reading, he suggested that I report to Labor and Delivery as soon as possible. He told me to get checked in and he would follow up with me at the hospital later that afternoon.

I was becoming *preeclamptic*. In other words, my kidneys were not functioning well enough to filter out the protein that my body was producing. A trace of protein is not too alarming, but the hospital needed to test my urine over the next 24-hour period in order to make sure that my kidneys were not in fact failing. An elevated blood pressure is also a symptom of preeclampsia and by itself can be managed medically—but with my kidneys not filtering correctly the situation was distressing.

I was admitted immediately. Shortly after I was settled in my room, I began to panic. Maybe it was because I was faced with so similar a situation as my first pregnancy and the fact that I was nine weeks from my due date, which still seemed so far away. I had read about preeclampsia in many pregnancy books and it is a serious condition even though fairly common. The cure to preeclampsia is preterm delivery of the infant, plain and simple.

Dr. Ambrose helped us see the situation from his viewpoint. The good, the bad and the ugly were: *the good*, Korri was a lot older than Kobe. At thirty-one weeks, her lungs were developed and she was spending the remainder of her time in the womb simply putting on more weight. *The bad*: I may have to deliver another preemie. At nine weeks early there was still quite a bit of risk for a baby so small. Besides, all that I could think of was losing another baby and I was not ready for the grief and heartache again. *The ugly*: We found out the following afternoon that the 24-hours of urine testing yielded protein levels that had increased to seven times what was normal. If Korri stayed inside, the blood vessels to the placenta would shut down and soon she would not receive anything from me while I carried her. With the last issue being the primary one, Dr.

Ambrose made the order for the immediate labor and delivery of our daughter, Korri.

On August 19, 2001 at 2:30 p.m., I was induced with petocin. Labor began for Andy, Korri and I. I felt numb that day because of the familiar worries that started to creep back into my soul. I prayed, but could not understand why I was in this predicament again. I was not sure what the Lord's purpose was for me and Andy. I struggled again with believing that He loved me.

At 6:30 p.m. on August 20 (nearly 28 hours later), Korri Faith Kay Slamans was born. She was 3 ½ pounds, 18 inches long, and absolutely precious. The most important thing about her delivery was that she cried! It was the most beautiful sound that I had ever heard. Compared to Kobe's silent, uneventful birth, Korri's was loud and as the doctors checked her over (in my room!), she wailed angrily. I laughed and kept asking Andy if that was our baby making all the noise. He nodded vigorously and grinned from ear to ear.

The nurse brought Korri over to me so that I could see her before she was taken to the NICU. I spoke to her softly and kissed her gently. Her eyes opened and she peeked at me because she knew my voice. I was delighted at her response and the fact that she was okay, but all too soon, she was taken from me and rushed to the seventh floor of the Medical Center where the hospital's children's ward was located. I could not go right away to be with her because I was given magnesium sulfate to lower my blood pressure during labor as well as an epidural right before delivery, so I was not in the best condition to get up and walk around.

Andy left me to see Korri shortly after she was admitted to the NICU. She was breathing in oxygen through a tube when Andy first went in. Her "crib" was a transparent plastic isolette and there were monitors reporting Korri's vital signs through wires, which ran to her tiny body. The nurse's reports were positive, and their main concern was preparing for Korri's first feeding.

A preemie's bowels are highly sensitive because their bodies are not ready to digest food. In fact, preemies do not learn to "eat" by mouth until approximately 34 weeks along, so her first feeding and digestion needed to be attempted soon and the nurses were relying on my breast milk. Korri would have a feeding tube inserted into her mouth and it would run down her throat to her stomach cavity.

When Andy returned to my room, he was both excited and nervous for Korri. I was not sure what to feel—joy, fear, or hope. She seemed okay when she left the room, so when Andy asked me for some milk to take back down to her I looked at him dumbly because I had not even thought to prepare to feed my baby. This was all new to me, and I think I was still gearing up for bad news. I honestly did not believe that she would make it past the first few hours after she was born. But, apparently, I had new reason to hope.

Charged with renewed vigor, I mentally and emotionally geared myself up to be a mom. When the pain medicine and numbness left my system, I ventured up to the seventh floor to see my baby daughter. Andy pushed me in a wheelchair because I still felt light-headed off and on whenever I stood. He instructed me where to enter the Intensive Care Unit and, once inside, showed me how to scrub for fifteen minutes, from fingertips to elbows. We used the same antiseptic soap that doctors use prior to going in to surgery.

When we entered the area of beds where Korri was lying, I noticed that the lights were turned down low. It was not because all of the babies were sleeping. Preemies have many medical needs, one of which is a need for very little stimulation. In fact, too much interaction will cause them to lose weight because—though born, they are not full-term babies. The way the nurses considered their personal surroundings was ingenious. I took note during our first few visits, that we could only hold Korri for fifteen minutes at a time. Longer visits would cause her to lose weight.

Music was not played in the NICU and at night, the lights were always dimmed.

There were so many tubes attached to Korri that it was difficult to "hold" her, so whenever Andy and I wanted to touch or rub her, the nurse showed us how to open the two round windows to her isolette. She demonstrated how to firmly hold, with one hand, her bottom (which was up in the air--her feet tucked under her) and, with the other hand, hold her head still. We were told that this tight hold is comforting to preemies because it feels very much like the womb. I loved to see Andy's large hands around Korri.

During my first visit, Andy placed his large hands around her, and he prayed for her as she lay sleeping in her isolette. She was wearing a small preemie outfit supplied by the hospital. There were the teeniest booties on her feet and a knit hat on her head. Underneath, her hair was dark and smoothed down straight. She was off the oxygen, but was still breathing in room air from a tube. I saw with my own eyes that she was in fact doing fine.

The day that I was discharged from the hospital, I had mixed emotions. Again, I was faced with the reality of leaving the hospital without my newborn baby. I felt resentment creep in and a sense of helplessness because I did not want to leave Korri behind. After we left the hospital, I busied myself at home and at the store purchasing supplies for my little preemie daughter. I bought Korri the most darling preemie clothes to wear and it was exciting for me. I also had to pump my milk, freeze it, and transport it to the hospital via a small cooler, so I worked to get on Korri's regular feeding schedule. It was good for me to keep myself occupied as I spent my first day home getting together all that I needed for my return visit to the hospital.

Every night, during the first week of Korri's life, I prayed desperately for her to stay alive long enough for me to gaze on her beautiful face the next morning. Even though the nurses were very optimistic and reassured me that she was doing well, I had this overwhelming dread that would not leave me. I feared the worst—that she would die sometime during the night and I would not be there with her. I often cried myself to sleep—sick with worry.

Every morning, after Andy got the boys off to school, we made the journey to the hospital's seventh floor. After a few days, we were regulars there and our routine of scrubbing up to our elbows was commonplace. Silently we would push the glass doors aside and enter the area of the hospital where life was the most delicate.

One particular morning, when we reached Korri's bed, we saw that she did not have any clothes on except for a mostly see-through diaper. There was a sign over her tiny bed that said she was having a beach day, and there was a bright lamp on over her. She had patches shielding her eyes from the light and her name was written on a sign with a beach umbrella and sunglasses drawn in bright colors. It was the hospital's way of gently telling us that she had jaundice. They also told us not to worry.

When I asked the nurse if any other complications had developed, she stated that overall, Korri's progress was good, and only the jaundice was what they were concerned with at that point. Previously, she had to overcome sleep apnea, and the hospital staff treated it with a small dose of caffeine. This treatment allowed the babies to sleep, but not too soundly, as they would often stop breathing in deep sleep.

During our feeding sessions, Korri and I got the rare opportunity to bond. Even though she had a feeding tube running to her stomach, emotionally, she connected her filling stomach to my face. We were highly encouraged to be present—and to hold her during her feedings. Korri was too small to suck, breathe, and swallow all at the same time, but we knew that this skill would develop for her in a few weeks.

For the time being, Andy held her as often as I did so that she could gaze into his eyes and take in his friendly smile and gentle voice. I made sure to be at the hospital for her daytime and evening feedings and spent much of the day there pumping, freezing, thawing and heating milk for Korri. I also got the opportunity to bathe Korri after most of the tubes were disconnected from her. It was an emotional few weeks, but slowly peace overshadowed my worries as I learned how to care for my delicate little princess.

On the morning of September 11, 2001--Andy and I woke and went about our day as usual. I realized later on that I had not turned on the television set at all that morning. At around 9:30 am, when we arrived at the hospital, we took the elevator up to the Children's Hospital as was our usual routine. When we entered the waiting room, everyone was standing up; facing the television monitors which were cranked up at high volume. CNN played on one of the sets and the others were tuned to various local news stations. All showed live feeds to New York City's Financial District. Watching, Andy and I learned quickly what drew everyone's attention: someone had flown an airplane into one of the Twin Towers located in New York City.

We stood there in awe as we watched repeated accounts of what had taken place just an hour before. One of the towers was on fire and images of yet another airplane flying into the second tower kept played over and over on a split screen. Then, as all eyes were on New York, the second tower began to collapse. Screams came across the television speakers and gasps were heard all around the waiting room area. The first tower that was hit was still standing. Commentators began to shout as they relayed what was unfolding before my eyes. I was alarmed and confused at what had happened. Terrorists had not been given the credit yet for what was taking place. Everyone thought it was one huge accident. Whatever it was, I knew that it was horribly wrong.

I immediately thought of my twin sister who was living in New York. I was not sure where she was working, but I knew that she was probably aware of the situation just as we were. As we scrubbed up for our visit to see Korri, Andy and I talked about what had happened. We overheard doctors and nurses talking in hushed voices about family and friends who lived and worked around the Twin Towers. I saw fear on the faces of many that day and I said a silent prayer for my sister.

I rushed to Korri's bedside and scooped her up. Andy and I held onto her tightly. That morning we had discovered how cruel our world could be and I dared not let her go. As tiny as she was, her life brought me comfort, but it also made me afraid. I was not ready for how great my desire to protect her became. My fear of losing her grew that day and it increased in the years that followed. Only a loving God could help loosen the grip that this fear held over me.

CHAPTER EIGHT

I love the Lord because His word is timeless and ageless. He is called the Ancient of Days and He knows the hearts of men in all of our walks of life. Because I did not grow up in the church, I have the peculiar benefit of looking at God's Word with fresh eyes. Sunday school stories have their place, but if they are taken simply at face value when we are young, we will miss so much of what the Lord wants to show us as we grow with Him.

Of the most profound stories I have ever read in scriptures, the Lord's story of Abraham's test with Isaac has meant more to me over the past ten years than any other story. I never tire of reading God's word because of the new truths He brings to me, if I take the time to search them out. In Genesis 22:1-12, we read this very troubling account about how God tested Abraham.

Some time later God tested Abraham. He said to him, "Abraham!"

"Here I am," he replied.

Then God said, "Take your son, your only son Isaac, whom you love, and go to the region of Moriah. Sacrifice him there as a burnt offering on one of the mountains I will tell you about."

Early the next morning, Abraham got up and saddled his donkey. He took with him two of his servants and his son, Isaac. When he had cut enough wood for the burnt offering, he set out for the place God had told him about. On the third day, Abraham looked up and saw the place in the distance. He said to his servants, "Stay here with the donkey while I and the boy go over there. We will worship and then we will come back to you."

Abraham took the wood for the burnt offering and placed it on his son Isaac and he himself carried the fire and the knife. As the two of them went on together, Isaac spoke up and said to his father Abraham, "Father?"

"Yes, my son?" Abraham replied.

"The fire and the wood are here," Isaac said," but where is the lamb for the burnt offering?"

Abraham answered, "God Himself will provide the lamb for the burnt offering my son." And the two of them went on together.

When they reached the place God had told him about, Abraham built an altar there and arranged the wood on it. He bound his son Isaac and laid him on the altar, on top of the wood. Then he reached out his hand and took the knife to slay his son. But the angel of the Lord called out to him from heaven, "Abraham! Abraham!"

"Here I am," he replied.

"Do not lay a hand on the boy," he said. "Do not do anything to him. Now I know that you fear God, because you have not withheld from me your son, your only son."

This haunts believers because many times we wonder why a loving God would ask so much of Abraham simply as a test. However, when we ask God to show us what He wants for our lives specifically, we can learn so much from these Biblical stories. I bring this passage to the forefront because, like Abraham, I have felt God's tug on my heart to journey with Him to a deeper level—to walk with Him a little further, to linger with Him longer as He helps me to climb higher. Just as Abraham's "Isaac" represented His *faith* in the Lord, likewise, my "Isaac" represented my *trust* in Him—and the Lord used both Kobe and Korri to show me how I needed to trust Him more.

When Korri eventually came home from the hospital on September 21, 2001, I clung to her (and Andy) in an unhealthy way. I knew that it was unhealthy because I was still convinced that somehow I would lose her to some unpredictable freak accident or illness. As the years went on, I continued to have reservations about carrying another child. I thought for sure that I had better not "push" it with God and even think of another pregnancy. I figured He had given us Korri and at two years old she was an absolute doll and a joy to raise. She suffered nothing developmentally even though she was born a preemie. She was beautiful and as an added bonus, well-behaved. But, deep down perhaps I was still longing for that boy that I lost four years earlier.

One evening, while I was working through a prayer journal authored by Beth Moore, called *Whispers of Hope*[3], I stumbled upon a poem that she had written regarding Abraham's sacrifice. As I read, it dawned on me that Beth had captured in words the very doubts and fears that I had yet to let go of. Up until that point, I did not release the intensity in which I held onto Korri, and the discovery of this alarmed me.

For every Abraham who dares to kiss a foreign field where glory for a moment grasped is for a lifetime tilled...

The voice of God speaks not but once but 'til traveler hears "Abraham! Abraham! Bring your Isaac here!"

"Bring not the blemished sacrifice. What lovest thou the most? Look not into the distance, you'll find your Isaac close."

"I hear the tearing of your heart torn between two loves, the one your vision can behold the Other hid above."

"Do you trust me, Abraham with your gravest fear?
Will you pry your fingers loose and bring your Isaac here?"

"Have I not made you promises? Hold *them* tight instead! *I* am the Lover of your soul—the Lifter of your head."

"Believe me, O my Abraham when blinded by the cost. Arrange the wooded altar and count your gains but loss."

"Let tears wash clean your blinded eyes until unveiled you see—the ram caught in the thicket there to set your Isaac free."

"Perhaps I'll send him down the mount to walk right by your side. No longer in your iron grasp but safer still in mine."

"Or I may wrap him in the wind and sweep him from your sight to better things beyond your reach—believe with all your
might!"

"Look up, beloved Abraham. Can you count the stars?
Multitudes will stand to reap from one dear friend of God."

**"Pass the test, my faithful one; bow to *me* as Lord.
Trust me with your Isaac—see, I am your great Reward."**

It was one thing to offer up Kobe, because I simply had no choice. But, at that moment I heard the Lord ask me if I would take Kobe back in exchange for Him? It was a question that I stuttered to answer. Then I knew that I was holding on too tight to Kobe's death, Korri's life, Andy and everything else that I had used as my security.

Right then I learned to give Korri up as a *living* sacrifice to the Lord. I could no more hold onto Korri as I could Kobe even with her in my arms. She was the Lord's even though He had given her to us to raise. I've often heard people say your children are on loan from the Lord. But, for someone like me, who had lost so much, it has never been a comforting piece of advice.

That day, God's voice was a gentle rebuke for me to get my priorities in line and to finally trust Him with *everything* He had given me. I prayed and asked the Lord to show me how to trust Him with Korri and to give up worrying obsessively about her well-being. This was the first of so many things that God wanted to show me about Him. It was also the first time since Kobe's death that I desired to see what He wanted to do in me through this situation.

~~~~~~

I did not have to wait long. As soon as I opened my heart to the possibility that God could turn good out of Kobe's death, He began to show me so much of Himself. One particular Sunday, while Andy and I were attending church, the pastor began a new sermon series entitled, "Healing the Offended Heart". It was, in essence, a series on forgiveness. The initial sermons were on dealing with offenses done by our neighbors, family members, and even the church. The teachings were profound and throughout the months that followed, I did a personal inventory of my life, making sure that I had not been hung up somewhere along the way with hidden unforgiveness in my heart.

Even though Andy and I had not attended church for all of the messages, there was a common thread that ran through them—hidden or undiscovered offenses hinder the work of the Holy Spirit in a Believer's life. I enjoyed the sermons and even downloaded some messages on the computer if we were working a particular Sunday and could not make the service. However, on Sunday, November 11, 2003, Andy and I were able to be at church for the last sermon of the series. I knew that the Lord designed the message specifically for me a few minutes after the pastor began, and I also knew that I would never be the same again after hearing that message because it profoundly changed my life.

The pastor spoke out of Philippians 4:4-7 that morning, and he challenged us about the most subtle of offenses: *being offended with God.* I knew as I sat and listened, that I would have to make a life changing decision. Before that day I had not put words to the wall that stood between me and the Lord. But on that morning, I knew that the wall was me keeping score through the many disappointments that God had allowed to take place in my life. It was a completely twisted view of Jesus, but when the pain is intense, often we see Jesus in a skewed way. The wall that I began building when I was very small, was indeed distorting my view and it had to be torn down if I was to be truly free. I needed to put behind me for the last time, the worries that plagued me and all the hurts from my past that kept me from giving the Lord my *whole* heart.

As I listened to the sermon, I also knew that there was a wound there that came from me wanting another child. I had carried around with me for so long this false belief that God did not love me enough to give me another child without some kind of hardship. This thinking prevented me from asking Him with confidence. I had concluded that day that I had sin in my heart that had not been dealt with and it was getting in the way of my relationship with the Holy Spirit. It was the sin of unbelief and the sin of pride, thinking that God somehow owed me an explanation.

When the sermon ended, we were all challenged to deal with this last and most subtle offense. I went forward, told a woman from the prayer team my need, and I wept uncontrollably, but prayed expectantly. I had faith when I prayed because I knew that this was true freedom in Christ—to no longer be bound by life's circumstances, but to trust God *no matter what.*

That afternoon, when I got home, I prayed to get pregnant. I prayed for a long time and hoped God would say "yes". I also knew that if the answer was "no", that I would be all right because I had finally begun to accept the Lord's sovereignty in so many ways.

Now, almost five years after that life-changing moment with God, I have another son named "AJ" (Andrew Jeremiah) who is three years old. He was born on March 12, 2005. I carried him on bed rest, just as I did the two before him, but this time I made it all the way to 38 weeks. My pregnancy with him was a joyous one. Not once, while

I carried him, did I battle doubt, fear, or depression. Even today, the peace that entered my spirit when I gave over my offenses to the Lord is still with me.

Andrew Jeremiah, in turn, is the happiest little boy I have ever met. His smile melts hearts—even when he gets into trouble. Whenever I see his grin and his twinkling eyes, I think of his father's smile and the sparkle that I noticed in his eyes that set off the spark in our relationship. I also think of the joy that the Lord has given me because it comes from the trust that is finally growing in my heart.

The following year—the year that we celebrated Korri's fifth birthday, AJ's first birthday and Kobe's seventh—the Lord spoke to me a final word regarding my children's pregnancies. It was in the morning during my prayer time that I was reflecting on Kobe turning seven and what all that the number seven means to the Lord. I had heard before, that the number stands for "completion" or "fullness". God uses the number 7 for the days he created the world. He also uses it for the Sabbath day and even the many things that were practiced in the Levitical Law were to take place in the seventh month.

With that in mind, I felt that God was saying to me that my journey with Him in this area was complete and that He had accomplished His purpose. However, I was not certain that God meant this for me until He confirmed in my spirit *what* He had made complete in my life. The illustration in my mind that followed was an amazing picture of God's grace and mercy. I had not noticed before that day that I had carried Korri seven weeks longer than I had Kobe, and that I had carried AJ seven weeks longer than I had Korri. I believe the Lord wanted to show me this to confirm in my heart that He wants to be involved in every area of my life—even to the tiniest detail. I was amazed that God took the time to show me this.

Surprisingly, only a few months after receiving this revelation, I was called upon to minister to a friend who had just delivered her daughter--stillborn. When I received the phone call about the news, the words from a friend that were spoken on the other end made everything crystal clear: *Deanna, you are the only person I could think of to call because you understand what she is going through.* Unfortunately, my friend was correct. I knew that after all the years of wrestling with God and praying my children into existence, and then letting them go, that He was faithful--especially when life was unpredictable and painful.

I decided to meet with this grieving mother as soon as possible. As I cried, and prayed, and listened to this mother's broken heart, I saw myself seven years earlier in her tear-stained face. I knew that she had a journey with

God to overcome and I prayed that it would prove fruitful. Not too long after that, I received news from another friend that she had lost her child at eighteen weeks' gestation. I met with this woman also to show her God's truths even in the midst of pain and loss. As I spoke of the Lord, He brought even more comfort to my heart.

Many times, if we are brave enough, we must share our hurts so that others can be healed. Paul encourages this in 2 Corinthians 1:3-7: *Praise be to the God and Father of our Lord Jesus Christ, the Father of compassion and the God of all comfort, who comforts us in all our troubles, so that we can comfort those in any trouble with the comfort we ourselves have received from God. For just as the sufferings of Christ flow over into our lives, so also through Christ our comfort overflows.*

Was this the purpose that God had for me? His glory was being revealed in the strangest way. It is through all of our hurts that He is most glorified. Even in His glory he takes a humble approach and uses our suffering to show His power. This year of completion showed me all that God was preparing to do. I wondered at His goodness as I watched Him turn a bad situation into healing for others and me. I was also reminded how close He was to my broken heart and how He saved me when I was crushed in spirit.

Part Three

"...They will be called Oaks of Righteousness, a planting of the Lord for the display of his splendor."—Isaiah 61:3b

CHAPTER NINE

Presently, I am sitting on the back porch outside of my apartment at the Milton Hershey School. After almost nine years, Andy and I have continued to work at this marvelous place. This particular spot has become a wonderful place to write. In the distance is a huge tree where Andy has tied a tire swing for the kids. They love to swing. Even the ever-growing boys in our home will wander over there every once and awhile and get lost in their childhood. I can also see the back of the next-door neighbor's student home. The couple that works there have become dear friends. Other than that, trees are my sanctuary as I draw this memoir to a close. This has been an intense journey—but then again, reliving the most painful and monumental moments in life, is intense. However, if the Lord gives you the bravery to embark on this kind of road for healing, it is worth the trip.

One particular passage that I like to meditate on, when I sit on my back porch can be found in the book of Isaiah. The first three verses of chapter 61 have become my life verses. These words are the same ones that Christ spoke at the beginning of His ministry not too long after Satan tempted him.

The Spirit of the Sovereign Lord is on me,

because the Lord has anointed me

to preach good news to the poor.

He has sent me to bind up the broken hearted,

to proclaim freedom for the captives

and release for the prisoners,

to proclaim the year of the Lord's favor

and the day of vengeance of our God,

to comfort all who mourn,

and provide for those who grieve in Zion—

to bestow on them a crown of beauty instead of ashes,

the oil of gladness instead of mourning

and a garment of praise instead of a spirit of despair.

They will be called oaks of righteousness,

a planting of the Lord for the display of His splendor.

I love Isaiah's book because not only does he have the most references to Christ's prophetic birth, death and resurrection, of all of the prophets, but, His book has contained profound wisdom for me as I have discovered the Lord's heart among its pages.

Over the years, I have had the pleasure of singing Crystal Lewis's song, *Beauty for Ashes*, whenever Andy or I share the story of my childhood. It is an amazing song taken from this very chapter in Isaiah's book. The words in the text are astounding and the promises in it bring chills to me every time that I read them.

Growing up with so much loss and unexplainable crises, I realize that it takes bravery to look my brokenness in the face and give it some names. I have found that many of the words in the text are all too familiar to the cries of my own heart. When I choose to identify with the words: *mourning, grief, despair, broken hearted,* and *captivity,* I find hope and joy in Christ who promises to bind my wounds, free and comfort me and bring beauty into what was otherwise an ugly life.

One of the many results, however, of growing up with tragic and unpredictable events so early in life, is the tendency to develop long-lasting, unhealthy issues that are difficult to overcome. My defense mechanism to a chaotic childhood was the need to be a high performer or overachiever. When the pain became too great for me, I threw myself into my work, my activities and anything else I could to escape the world that was falling down around me.

The problem with someone using performance as a place to hide is, at some point you will fail—and during those times that I did, I fell hard. Disappointed children are familiar with the pain that others can heap on their shoulders, but they often cannot understand their own shortcomings. It becomes the thing that they fear the most—letting someone or themselves down...and when it happens, it is devastating.

Even after I became a Christian, I battled this faulty thinking for a very long time. The very thing that I resented in my parents and upbringing, I saw in myself— imperfection. I did not know how perilously close I was becoming to letting pride take up root in me. My pride was in my performance and it colored how I thought the Lord saw me. Year after year, I began to believe the lie that the accuser, Satan, began speaking to me. *You are not good enough for the Lord to use, so stop trying.* Fortunately, throughout this journey, the Lord continues to show me how He wishes to use me *in spite* of myself and when I focus on that I begin to feel the chains of bondage loosen some.

King David shows us poignantly after his discussion with Nathan, that the **quickest** way back to the Lord after a failure is the **only** way back to Him. In 2 Samuel 12, the prophet, Nathan, uses an illustration to expose King David's horrendous sins against Bathsheba and her husband, Uriah. When the eyes of David's heart are opened, he hears from the Lord and comes to repentance. I love his song of repentance found in the 51st Psalm. In particular, we read in verse 16: *You do not delight in sacrifice, or I would bring it; you do not take pleasure in burnt offerings. The sacrifices of God are a broken spirit; a broken and contrite heart, O God, you will not despise.*

David knew that his position with God was secure even though he messed up. He knew that brokenness is the exact place where God begins to use a fallen saint. David did not step down from his throne or cease talking with the Lord. Surprisingly, he fasted and prayed for the fate of his newborn son who was conceived illegitimately, hoping that God would somehow spare his life. His journey back to God's throne of grace was difficult, but he still found within his fragile heart a longing to approach Him. His desire to be in God's favor again is an amazing picture. What is even more astounding is the fact that David and Bathsheba later parent Solomon. He is the wisest man who ever lived, and he is the King who was given the privilege of building

God's holy temple. The Lord loves to redeem broken saints.

Oswald Chambers writes of this *Delight of Despair*[4] in his devotional dated May 24th:

It may be that like the apostle John you know Jesus Christ intimately, when suddenly He appears with no familiar characteristic at all, and the only thing you can do is to fall at His feet as dead. There are times when God cannot reveal Himself in any other way than in His majesty, and it is the awfulness of the vision that brings you to the delight of despair; if you are ever to be raised up, it must be by the hand of God...

Watch some of the things that strike despair. There is despair in which there is no delight, no horizon, no hope of anything brighter; but the delight of despair comes when I know that "in me (that is in my flesh) dwelleth no good thing..."

The group *Switchfoot*, on their *Beautiful Letdown* album has a song called *Dare You to Move*[5] that describes this tendency to stay frozen when we disappoint, and the restoration that can only happen when we dare to move towards Christ. It is powerfully accurate. Switchfoot's theology of restoration and repentance is biblical, but often not one that our fleshly hearts are ready to embrace. We tend to marinate in our failures in order to show the Lord how sorry we are, when the victorious life is one where we embrace Christ's victory and not Satan's accusations. A broken heart, like King David's, that knows it needs Christ is the only heart that God is interested in using.

Welcome to the planet...
Welcome to existence...
Everyone's here...
Everyone's here...
Everybody watches you now.
Everybody waits for you now.
What happens next?
What happens next?

I dare you to move
I dare you to move
I dare you to lift yourself up off the floor!
I dare you to move
I dare you to move
Like today never happened
Today never happened before!

Welcome to the fallout...
Welcome to resistance...
The tension is here...
The tension is here...
Between who you are and who you could be.
Between how it is and how it should be.

I dare you to move
I dare you to move
I dare you to lift yourself up off the floor!
I dare you to move

I dare you to move
Like today never happened
Today never happened...

Maybe redemption has stories to tell.
Maybe forgiveness is right where you fell.
Where can you run to escape from yourself?
Where you gonna go?
Where you gonna go?
Salvation is here.

Jesus speaks of this in His infamous Sermon on the Mount (Matthew 5) when His first words were: *Blessed are the poor in spirit, for theirs is the kingdom of heaven.* Those who are poor in spirit do not need their performance as their security, instead, they know that they need God, and it is a magnificent place to be.

CHAPTER TEN

Almost thirteen years ago, I had the pleasure and discomfort of being married. Marriage is uncomfortable because it allows for the uncanny nature of the spouses to play the role of "mirror" or "reflector" to one another. It is a most unpleasant thing to have someone show us our true selves—especially when that someone is the one that we love the most. Being married to Andy daily exposes the gaping hole that exists in my heart because I had an absent father and only a scant memory of my mother. Trying to grow in Christ without those childhood foundations, makes the hole even larger, and the pit sometimes feels bottomless. I know that there is a bottom whenever I remind myself that God loves me.

Before Andy, I never had to depend on a man for any length of time, to meet my needs. Growing up without a father, I had, for certain, no reference point for me to identify with the term "Heavenly "Father". I used to think that I could get by in our marriage without having to deal with this issue. After all, I was *independent. I had gotten this far at least, without much of my earthly father's help, right? So, why did I need to depend on Andy? I was an adult and had turned out fine.*

In the process, however, I was missing the childlike faith in Christ and in people that comes from what a stable family brings. In our marriage, early on, my heart was full of doubt that Andy had what it took to take care of our family and me. This lack of trust in God and Andy bore new scars and tore open old ones. Nevertheless, Andy was patient with me as I learned the slow process of trust.

I can remember recently, when Andy and I spoke fondly of his parents, a statement he said that shattered me to the core: He said, *you know, my parents have* never *let me down.* I screamed loudly in my head, *WHAT!?.* After thirteen years, I had never heard him say this. But obviously, after seeing his parents' marriage of 46 years, he is probably right. Absolutely they are not perfect, and there are things that his parents speak of often that they wished they had done much differently when they raised their sons. But, their commitment to each other, and their raising of four (now men) who are active in the church and faithfully married after 22, 20, 18, and our going on 13 years of marriage, is evident that many things went right in their family.

I have never seen this kind of faithfulness growing up. It is something that has taken up a bittersweet root in my heart. I love Andy's family because of their consistency and love of God. When we gather for holidays or vacations, we usually spend a few evenings praying and having devotions. Our most recent gathering was in Colorado and there were 23 of us in all. We shared stories of baptisms and memories of when we had come to Christ.

Again, I was in awe at the stability that this type of family can provide. To be a part of a stable family is water to my thirsty soul, and it also reminds me how much of an outsider I am when I think back on my childhood. I am grateful for these times because this bittersweet root is the motivation I need to make sure that I am as faithful to my family as Andy's parents were to theirs.

If our marriage brought to the surface my incompetence as Andy's soul mate, having children magnified it as a mother 100 times more! In particular, my relationship with my daughter Korri has been a beautiful and terrifying experience. Beautiful because when I had her, I felt for the first time that I could start over with my child and make sure that I "got it right" somehow. I loved taking care of her and being depended on as a mom. Korri's slate was clean, so to speak, in that she would not have to know first-hand any of the hardships that I had experienced growing up.

At seven, she is forming lasting memories of her parents together. There are tons of pictures of us as a family. I realize this must seem strange, but it is not when I think of the mere 30 pictures that I have of me as a child and the few with my mother in them. I cherish these photos deeply.

We teach Korri at home and we work together in the student home, so she and AJ get an extra-dose of their Mommy and Daddy almost all day. So far, Korri has not "wanted" for anything that she has desired except what we, as parents, draw firm limits on. She is learning how much God loves her and believes it with all of her heart. She is growing a heart to love and serve others as well.

Still, having a daughter is terrifying, because I have, in a sense, become a bridge between my mother and her. She is who I could have been if life dealt me a different hand. In a very real way, I wish that I could live my childhood over again and experience it the way that Korri is hers. I wish that what was not done right by me could be erased and I could have a second chance. However, because of what God plans were for me, my life has taken a different course. But I grieve the loss nonetheless.

Quite frankly, I have cried again and again for this little girl that is me, who never really was. Someone has to. It is not easy to give myself over to my pain. Only this year did

I really understand what it was that I was missing. She comes in the form of a beautiful little tan girl with a killer smile and curly hair. She is my daughter and she is *me*. She plays the piano and soccer. She is swung around in her father's strong arms and he doesn't put her down just because she's afraid. He laughs at her fear because he'll never drop her.

She is confident of her daddy's love and so she never questions God's. I know one day that she will. However, it will not come from a place of never knowing a father's love, someone, or something else will cause it. It is the fate of every man and woman, but for some reason, I know that it will not destroy her. She has a firm foundation already, and because of that I know she will be fine.

The movie, *Antwone Fisher* is a true story of an angry young man, who is filled with hate and pain and destruction. His hardened heart and explosive temper was created over a long period of time when his mother abandoned him after she delivered him in a state penitentiary. He was raised in the foster care system and experienced all manner of physical and emotional abuses. Yet he learned to deal with his losses with the help of his naval psychiatrist, Dr. Williams.

Andy and I have shown this movie to the boys in our student home over the years, to help them acknowledge their losses, grieve them, and move forward. Most of the boys at Milton Hershey School do not have a father present in their home of origin—if they know their father at all. We use this movie to help them gain a new awareness of who they are, but more importantly, through Christ, who they can become.

In the movie, a scene takes place during the holidays where Antwone is invited to the doctor's home for Thanksgiving dinner. Antwone takes in the familial essence that is in the room and the love of family that surrounds the table. After a short while he becomes overwhelmed and leaves the room. In private, he reads a poem that he wrote to the doctor and it is titled, *Who Will Cry for the Little Boy?* Whenever I read this poem, I pretend that it is the voice for every child who grew up hurt and ashamed. Every so often, I read it on behalf of myself and the students at Milton Hershey School so that my heart will remain tender towards the circumstances that we have all faced. The temptation to grow hard-hearted and cynical is too great.

Who Will Cry for the Little Boy?
by Antwone Q. Fisher

"Who will cry for the little boy,
lost and all alone?
Who will cry for the little boy,
abandoned without his own?

Who will cry for the little boy?
He cried himself to sleep.

Who will cry for the little boy?
He never had for keeps.

Who will cry for the little boy?
He walked the burning sand.

Who will cry for the little boy?
The boy inside the man.

Who will cry for the little boy?
Who knows well hurt and pain.

Who will cry for the little boy?
He died and died again.

Who will cry for the little boy?
A good boy he tried to be.

Who will cry for the little boy,
Who cries inside of me?"

If I was given a choice between what I have gained from living out my pain, even though I have come through it whole on the other side, and getting a second chance at childhood, I am afraid to say that the little girl in me still desires to relive things differently. I am grateful for all that I have and the insight that I have gained, but my short-sightedness wins out almost every time. Thankfully, God is ultimately the writer of my life story and not me. I am reminded anew that He knows what He is doing; and a glorified life in Christ is far better than a life of comfort and ease where there is no room for Him.

Even as I watch my husband raise Korri it is something that I almost cannot bear. Their relationship, still with all of its imperfections, is a wonder and does my heart good, but it brings to the surface, all of the loss and lack of memories as a child, that I have of my earthly father. Korri has learned from birth, what I never did, that her father is the man of her dreams, that the closest thing on earth to her Heavenly Father, is her earthly one, and that both are absolutely crazy about her.

She knows that she can depend on Andy to meet her needs: physically, emotionally, and spiritually and it is evident when she cries out and he is there for her every time. *He has never let her down.* Although she cannot see her Heavenly Father, she can equate warm feelings of Him because of the safety and dependence that Andy has provided when he comes through for her. This has been a delight to witness.

I know that for me, along with my sisters, this lack of a father figure has shown wear and tear on our lives. Our mother's early departure has marred our vision. We have not always seen things the ways that we should because the lenses of our hearts are scratched and torn. For the three of us, we have had to make some very difficult choices. With no one to guide us, we charted our own courses, and made mistakes along the way.

These choices have cost us dearly in one way or another. Knowing that we need God is not always enough of a conviction to move our hearts towards Him—especially if we do not know what He is like. I have often wondered, how then does one begin to fall in love with an *unfailing* God? The Lord is showing me that we do this by allowing an unfailing God to love us right where we are.

In Hebrews 13:5 we read a promise from God: *Never will I leave you, never will I forsake you.* Even in the midst of my failures as a broken vessel in constant need of mending, He is there and can handle my uncertainties. He knows my past, because He wrote it, so He holds the answers to my future…come what may. It is a journey of faith—of taking God at His word, *especially* when life screams otherwise.

This peace and security that Andy grew up seeing and knowing is the same peace that Christ is growing in my heart later in my life. Amazingly, it is the very peace that Andy and I wish to live out as we continue to work at MHS. We are reminded daily through ourselves and the students we work with, that Christ is still in the healing business and that His miracles did not stop when He died on the cross or when He was taken up to Heaven.

The devastation that comes from growing up in a broken home leaves scars and wounds that run deep. For the students in our care, Andy and I wish to be used of God to bring the oil of gladness to sad hearts, to preach good news to the poor, and to release captives. We want to plant seeds so that the Lord can grow up Oaks of Righteousness for His splendor and glory.

Yet, even as I desire this for our students, I am still learning that my redemption, healing, and freedom come at an awesome price: dying to myself continually so that Christ has total reign in my wounded spirit. Beth Moore, in her bible study entitled *Loving Well*[6] writes very poignant questions that every believer should use as a checkpoint when we are tempted to lose perspective of life when it goes in a different direction than we expected.

I learned how foreign love was to me in my life when I read these questions and basked in the wonder of these thoughts that God has towards me. As you read these questions, listen to the heart of God as He asks these of you:

Do you realize that I came to meet with you?

Do you have any idea how much I love you? How taken I am with you?

Do you know that I have never forsaken you nor will I ever reject you? I was there all along. I always will be.

Do you realize I knew everything about you the day you were conceived? I anticipated your life and planned for it.

You do have an enemy, My Child. But it is not Me. He wants you to think it is.

I am for you.

Do you think you need to prove yourself lovable to Me? Deep down inside, are you trying to earn My love and attention?

As you strive to love Me more, do you realize the key to loving Me more is to let Me love you more?

Why are you resisting Me? Why are you running from Me?

To whom have you compared Me, and with whom have you confused Me?

I'm not like them.

I know what's happened. I know what's on your mind.

I alone know the plan for how this turns out well. I alone know how to prosper you through this.

My eyes and My affections are on you right now.

Quit trying to be so strong. Let me be strong for you.

I love you unashamedly. Even now, My banner flies over you. Everyone in the Heavenlies knows how I feel about you. I'd leave you red-faced over My love for you...if you'd let Me.

I have only been able to love others well when I allow the Lord to love me *through* my hurts**, *in spite* of** my limits, and *because* He is love. My journey of faith has ultimately been one of acceptance. Acceptance of all God has allowed for me...acceptance of myself with all of my shortcomings and imperfections. Acceptance of this message He longs for me to share. Christ's love has shown me that when all else fails...*He does not.*

References

[1] Adapted from *My Utmost for His Highest*, pages 56-67. Oswald Chambers Publications Associations, Ltd., 1963. Uhrichsville, Ohio: Barbour and Company, Inc.

[2] Casting Crowns and *Voice of Truth*, MMII Provident Label Group, Inc. Franklin, Tennessee:

[3] Adapted from *Whispers of Hope*, by Beth Moore, pages 114-115. Nashville: Lifeway Press, 1998.

[4] Adapted from *My Utmost for His Highest*, pages 104-105. Oswald Chambers Publications Associations, Ltd., 1963.

[5] Switchfoot and *Dare You to Move, (C) 2004 SONY BMG MUSIC ENTERTAINMENT*

[6] *Who Will Cry for the Little Boy*, by Antwone Q. Fisher William Morrow Publishers, 2002.

[7] *Loving Well*, by Beth Moore, journal pages. Nashville: Lifeway Press, 2007.